Joseph Pearce

Violins and violin makers

Biographical dictionary of the great Italian artistes

Joseph Pearce

Violins and violin makers
Biographical dictionary of the great Italian artistes

ISBN/EAN: 9783337231880

Printed in Europe, USA, Canada, Australia, Japan

Cover: Foto ©Thomas Meinert / pixelio.de

More available books at **www.hansebooks.com**

VIOLINS
AND
VIOLIN MAKERS.

BIOGRAPHICAL DICTIONARY

OF THE

GREAT ITALIAN ARTISTES,

THEIR

FOLLOWERS AND IMITATORS,

TO THE

PRESENT TIME.

WITH ESSAYS ON IMPORTANT SUBJECTS
CONNECTED WITH THE VIOLIN.

BY JOSEPH PEARCE, JUN.

LONDON: LONGMAN AND CO., PATERNOSTER ROW.
SHEFFIELD: J. PEARCE, JUN.
1866.

ALDI PEARCE DISCIP.
SHEFFIELD.

CONTENTS.

	PAGE.
Preface	5
Introduction	8
Violin Makers, alphabetically arranged	15
Bow Makers	88
Cremona	93
Amati Family	93
Stradiuarius	107
On the Cremona Varnish	119
Guarnerius	121
Steiner	131
Why are certain Violins of more Value than others?	140
On the Production of Good Tone in Violins	148
Great Players and their Instruments	153
General Notes	155
Repairs of Instruments	161
Addenda	167

PREFACE.

The Violin is an instrument which, though small and of trifling original cost, has yet commanded most extraordinary prices. The reason of the immense difference in the value of these instruments must therefore be a subject possessing strong claims to notice from virtuoso and amateur.

To distinguish by the outward characteristics and peculiarities of tone, that which will be of pecuniary value to the possessor, and yield the utmost delight to the hearer, is an acquirement at once difficult to obtain and very valuable when obtained. To assist the amateur and collector in this pursuit is the object of the present little work. Such a work has long been a desideratum.

Of late years, the History of the Violin and its congeners has received much attention. Elaborate and costly treatises have been published, some of which being written in Foreign tongues, are exceedingly difficult to obtain, and not accessible to many of those who desire to peruse them, on that account. Others are very imperfect and unsatisfying. Others again, are, from their high price, beyond the reach of the greater number of amateurs.

The present work is intended chiefly for the use of those who desire a handy guide to the principal characteristics both of make and tone which mark the chief builders of this most famous instrument. Many persons anxious to possess a good instrument, and led away by the very natural desire to possess an Amati, a Guarnerius, or a Stradiuarius are tempted into purchasing Violins which are presented to them under false and delusive titles, and reject frequently good and genuine instruments of less famous makers, but still valuable because they are good and genuine. Undoubted specimens of the great masters are now very rarely to be had, unless at a very high price. Yet, when we consider that even Stradiuarius himself obtained no more than four pounds for his best instruments, which now command as many hundreds —it is evident that, in the absence of those great productions, the works of his pupils and successors are well worthy the attention of amateurs. There is no doubt, indeed, that many of these, which from being built on his principles are of first-rate quality, have been sold as those of the master himself. It cannot, therefore, be questioned that a knowledge which will lead the amateur to buy an instrument for what it really is, instead of what it professes to be, will at once save him from the unpleasantness of paying too dearly, and in real enjoyment yield all that can be desired.

The author believes he has in this work given the amateur and connoisseur information not easily attainable elsewhere, but as he is fully conscious that there may be imperfections in it still, he will be glad to receive any suggestions or information which may enable him to render it still more complete.

Sheffield, February, 1866.

INTRODUCTION.

The two most pleasing, expressive, and powerful single instruments of music are the human voice and the violin. The one, the gift of beneficent nature, has from the creation exercised its touching influence on the human soul—the other, the product of the ingenuity of man, has only within the last three centuries attained to perfection, but since that period what delight, what rapture has arisen from so simple a construction, when acted upon by the hand of genius!

While the melodious tones of Grisi and Mario have touched with sympathetic feelings the hearts and imaginations of spell bound listeners, how have the magic tones of Paganini and Ernst wrapped the souls of wondering thousands in an elysium of delight and admiration! What effect cannot be produced by the Violin, (except that of speech,) which the voice can accomplish?

The Violin in the hands of genius can draw tears or create laughter. Whoever has heard the great masters of this extraordinary instrument, has heard all the sweetness of tone, the intensity of feeling, the power of expression that the most gifted sons and daughters of song could possibly produce without the additional aid of speech. The Violin, in fact, in its power of expression far excels those singers, of whom there are too many, who while singing the notes, fail to make their hearers understand the sense of their songs. If a merry dance is produced by the agile bow, its sympathetic tones at once excite a corresponding feeling. If a plaintive air streams in delicious and heart-touching cadences from the strings, what soul is there so dead to feeling as not to respond?

The perfection of the Violin is that its master, if alive to the subtle and mysterious influences of the imagination, can elicit from it the most perfect and touching "songs without words."

It is besides the only instrument, except the voice, which is perfect. Every shade of expression, every nicety of tone can be produced on it. All other instruments sink into insignificance in comparison with the Violin, because they cannot do this. They are all more or less imperfect; and therefore fail in those subleties of expression of which the Violin and the voice are such able exponents.

What gratitude do we owe therefore to those great masters of Cremona, more especially the Amati and Stradiuarius, who have suceeded in bringing the Violin to its present state of perfection.

Music has in all ages been a source of the purest delight. The greatest poet and dramatist the world ever knew says that whoever " has not music in his soul is fit for treasons, stratagems, and spoils." In the present age the cultivation of Music forms one of the most general and the most refined sources of amusement and pleasure. All ranks of people are now privileged to join in its delightful enjoyments.

Even the cottage of the artisan is now often elevated by the elegant practice of music, through the increased facilities for producing instruments at a cheap rate. The consequence is that in the present age there is a more general study and a finer perception of what is good and beautiful, and their elevating tendencies are doing much for the mental cultivation and refinement of all classes.

A very extraordinary feature of the musical world of the present day is the enormous orchestras which can be produced on special occasions. A chorus of several thousand voices supported by hundreds of instruments may now be heard, rendering the immortal compositions of the greatest masters of the divine Art, in the Peoples' Palace at Sydenham and elsewhere. These Orchestras are chiefly selected from the ranks of the people, of whom the artisan is the chief contributor.

The reduction of the cost of instruments and the adoption of what may be called the joint stock principle are tending still further to enlarge the boundaries of the practical musical world. At any time and for any special purpose it is now easy to secure a band and chorus sufficient in numbers and executive power to render in an efficient and powerful manner, the glorious productions of Beethoven, Mozart, Handel, and other great masters.

In all these transitions, the Violin bears a most important part. It is the leading instrument in these great performances, as it is also, after the voice, the most powerful medium of expression in solo. It is also the peoples' instrument.

The labours of many eminent violin makers who have followed in the steps of the great masters have of late so immensely improved the art, that a good instrument may now be possessed by any one. And it may safely be said that with its improvement, has arisen also the extension and wide spread practice of music generally. An ear accustomed to the fine tone of a good violin will not now tolerate a bad piano-forte.

The Piano-forte and the Violin are the most general instruments, and they have alike participated in the improvements effected, in becoming cheaper by the advance of science. Every description of machinery has within the last fifty years received the attention of able men, and the mechanical construction of the Piano-forte is one prominent proof of the advantages which can be conferred by science on even the luxuries of life.

The Violin, also, seemingly the most incapable of mechanical application to its manufacture, is said to be now made by a most persevering and enthusiastic lover and follower of the great makers, by mechanical means. Copies of these celebrated makers, are now said to be manufactured by him with an uniformity, a certainty, and a precision impossible except by the aid of scientific improvements. These instruments are therefore understood to require only the ameliorating influences of time and use to become fine in tone and satisfactory in every respect.

Every one interested in the progress of music, must rejoice at the rapid development of its resources and the general spread of its pleasures among the people. We are a profoundly commercial nation, and it is delightful to see that in our greater wealth and prosperity, rational amusements, and more especially music, go on increasing step by step with our more business-like occupations. This class of amusements must exercise a humanising and refining influence on the habits and manners of the people, and they should be, therefore, patronised and encouraged by all those whose means are large and their example powerful. There can be no doubt that their tendency is for good, and that those whose leisure hours are devoted to their practice and study, will be richly benefited by them in all those qualities which combine to make the good citizen and the estimable friend.

NOTE.

To prevent too much space being taken up in the alphabetical portion of this work, separate chapters are given on the four renowned Violin Makers, Amati, Stradiuarius, Guarnerius and Steiner. The names and dates of each of the members of these celebrated families are however given in their proper places, for prompt reference.

We have not in some cases been able to find any records beyond the names of certain makers. Wherever possible we have given dates, places, and style of work.

DICTIONARY
OF
VIOLIN MAKERS.

A.

ACEVO, —— Cremona, Pupil of Guiseppe Cappa. This artiste made very good violins in the style of the Amati.

ADDISON, WILLIAM, London, 1670.

AIRETON, EDMUND, London, 1730.
 A good and neat Maker.

ALDRED, —— London,
 Early English Lute Maker.

ALETZIE, PAULO, Monaco, 1720-30.
 Famous for his Violoncellos.

ALBANI, MATTHIAS, born at Botzen or Bulsani, in the Tyrol, about 1621. This artist was highly esteemed formerly, and Otto says that it is exceedingly difficult to give so exact a description of them as readily to distinguish them from those of Nicholas Amati, who was said to be his master. In the present day, opinions are very different. Nevertheless there are some fine instruments by this maker, of high model, with reddish brown varnish and bearing a great similarity to those of Steiner, of whom he was also said to be a pupil. The "Dictionary of Musicians" speaks highly of this maker. This was decidedly the best artiste of this name.

ALBANI, PAOLO, Palermo and Cremona,
Was also under Nicholas Amati, about 1659.

ALBANI, —— son of the above, about 1712, was also a careful maker, and turned out some good Instruments.

AMATI FAMILY,
For fuller particulars of these eminent makers, see separate Article.

AMATI, ANDREAS, Cremona, born 1520, died 1580.

AMATI, NICHOLAS, brother of the above, celebrated for his Basses.

AMATI, NICHOLAS, son of Andreas,

AMATI, ANTONIUS and HIERONYMUS.
Sons of Andreas, 1550 to 1634, first made together and afterwards separately.

AMATI, NICHOLAS, born 1596, died 1684, son of Heironymus. This was the greatest maker of the Family.

AMATI, ANTONIO JEROME, do.
1640 to 1670.

AMATI, HIERONYMUS, Son of Nicholas, born 1649, said to be the last of the Amati family. A violin of his is mentioned, dated 1672.

AMELINGUE, —— Paris, 18th Century.

ANSELMO, PIETRO, Venezia, 18th Century

ARTMANN, GOTHA.
Followed Cremona pattern.

ASSALONE, GASPARD, Rome,
18th Century. Cremona patterns.

B.

BACHMANN, LOUIS CHARLES,
Berlin, born 1716, died 1800. Considered to be one of the best makers of Germany. Otto says, the Instruments by this Maker are next in point of quality to the Cremonese. Without going so far, with our present increased knowledge of the pupils of the Cremona makers, it may still be admitted that Bachmann was an exellent maker and was very careful in his proportions, so that Amateurs have been often deceived into thinking them genuine Cremonas. They

are of the flat Stradiuarius Model, made of good wood, with amber varnish, and therefore present considerable similarity to their patterns.

BAGANZI, —— see Bergonzi.

BAGATELLA, PIETRO,—Padua, 1766.
Said not to be very good.

BAGATELLA, ANTONIO,—Padua, 1782.
Author of a Work on the construction of Instruments, from which Bishop in his Translation of Otto, has appended a Theory for making a Violin on a very simple plan. He made some excellent Violins after Cremona patterns.

BAINES, —— London, about 1780.

BAKER, —— Oxford about 1720.

BALESTRIERI, THOMAS,
This excellent Maker was a pupil of Stradiuarius, and made after his model, The Author has seen an Instrument by this Artist, which is of the large flat pattern and has a magnificent and brilliant tone. The wood of the back and ribs rather plain—the belly very fine open grain, purfling not very neat—varnish reddish

yellow. Pronounced by judges to be equal to a fine Stradiuarius. It is dated Thomas Balestrieri, Cremonensis, fecit Mantua, 1757. This instrument is a proof that amateurs may in future look with safety to the pupils of Stradiuarius for violins to take the place of those of the great masters, which are yearly becoming scarcer and dearer.

BALESTRIERI, PIETRO, Cremona,
rather earlier than Thomas.

BANKS, BENJAMIN,   Salisbury.
Born 1727, died 1795. Foster in his excellent work calls him "one of England's best manufacturers. Too much cannot be said in praise of this justly celebrated Maker. The work of all the better class of instruments is excellent, the tone good of all; but that of the Violoncellos in particular is full and sonorous." Mr. Gardiner in his " Music and Friends," says " Banks of Salisbury's Violoncellos are of the finest quality of tone—not so strong and fiery as Foster's, but in sweetness and purity excelling them." They are chiefly of the Amati pattern.—The best Instruments have

brownish yellow Varnish with a tinge of red, others deep red of a blackish tinge, Varnish not brilliant.

BANKS, BENJAMIN, Son of the former, London, born 1754, died 1820.

BANKS, JAMES and HENRY, Salisbury, other sons of the same. James is said to have been an excellent workman in his father's style, and dates about 1805.

BARRETT, JOHN, London, about 1725.

His labels state him to live at the Harp and Crown, in Picadilly. He made some good instruments, but did not purfle them. The author has seen a Violoncello by this maker which was everything that could be desired in the matter of tone. The wood and workmanship, however, were not equal to the tone, and this circumstance will probably partly account for the settled preference now given to the Italian instruments over all the old English makers.

BARTON, GEORGE, London, died 1810.

BEKMAN, SWENO, Stockholm, 1706.

BELLOSIO, ―――― one of the Venetian makers, 18th Century.

BENOIST, —— Paris, 18th Century.

BENTE, MATTEO, Brescia, about 1580.
Well known among virtuosi as a maker of merit in the style of Gaspar di Salo and Magini.

BERGONZI, or BAGANZI, FRANCISCO, Cremona, 1687.

BERGONZI, CARLO, Cremona, 1712 to 1750,
Considered by authorities to be the best pupil of Stradiuarius. He made instruments of the same beautiful and brilliant tone which has rendered the productions of his master famous throughout the world. Constructed on similar principles, and generally of well-chosen wood, there is no doubt the productions of this excellent artiste will hereafter rank very high. Like Stradiuarius himself, Carlo Bergonzi is by some considered to have been at one time a pupil of Nicholas Amati. Every amateur would, if it were possible, get a Stradiuarius, an Amati, or a Guarnerius, but as the genuine violins of these makers are very rare and valuable, they should

look for the veritable instruments of their pupils, which are now beginning to be highly esteemed on account of their intrinsic excellence.

BERGONZI, NICHOLAS,
Son of Carlo, but said to be inferior to his father.

BERGONZI, MICHAEL ANGELO,
Probably another son of Carlo. He, also, has the credit of being a pupil of Stradiuarius, though that seems rather doubtful, because the latter died in 1737, at which time, if a son of Carlo, he would not have been old enough.

BERNADEL, —— Paris, 18th Century.

BETTS, JOHN, called Old Betts, London.
and
BETTS, EDWARD, his nephew.
These two well known makers were said to be pupils of Duke, but often employed other artistes, such as Carter, Panormo, B. Fendt, and his sons, whose work, chiefly imitations of the Cremona instruments, gained them great reputation both at home and abroad. 1782 to 1823.

BINTERNAGLE,—— Gotha, 18th Century.
   This maker was a German imitator of the Cremona Violins, and is said to have been very successful.

BOCQUAY, JAQUES, Paris, about 1620.
   A very good maker, and highly esteemed in France.

BODIO, —— Venezia, 18th Century.

BOLLES, ——
   An early English Lute and Viol Maker. Mace, 1675, says "one bass of Bolles, I have known valued at £100," equal to at least £600 of our present money.

BORELLI, ANDREAS, Parma, 1740.

BOULLAINGER, —— London.
   A careful maker, who first worked for others, and now on his own account.

BREMEISTER, JAN., Amsterdam, 1707.

BROSCHI, CARLO, Parma, 1744.

BRETON ᴸe) Paris.

BROWN 'MES, born 1670, died 1834.

and

BROWN, JAMES, son of do., born 1786, died 1860. Both good workmen, but without any speciality.

BUCHSTADTER,—Ratisbon. 18th Century. Used the flat model. Otto says the wood is not good, and therefore, though well built, the tone is not fine; but Spohr puts his violins on his list as excellent instruments. He may, therefore, be ranked among the good German makers.

BUDIANI, JAVIETTA, Brescia, about 1580. Made after the style of Gaspar di Salo.

C.

CAESTA, PIETRO ANTONIO DELLA, Trevisa, 18th. Century, imitated Stradiuarius.

CAMILE, CAMILUS de, Mantua, esteemed as a pupil of Stradiuarius.

CAPPA, GIACHIMO or GIOFREDA or probably two Brothers, born at Cremona and worked under Amati. Date there about 1590 and were in Piedmont 1640.

There are some good Violoncellos of this make.

CAPPA, GUISEPPE—Saluzzo—end of 16th Century.

CAPPER,——— or probably Cappa, Mantua. A Violin of this make was sold by auction in London in 1861, and said to be very good.

CARTER, JOHN, London, 1789, made some excellent instruments which were sold both under his own name and under that of John Betts for whom he had worked.

CARLO, GUISEPPE, Milan 1769.

CASSINO, ANTONIO, Modena, 17th Century

CASTAGNERY, JEAN PAUL, Paris 1639 to 1662. This artist is considered to be one of the best of the old French Makers. One authority says they have a fine silvery tone but not powerful.

CASTAGNERI, ANDREA, Paris. 18th Century.

CHANOT, —— Mirecourt, France, a good maker, 18th Century.

CHANOT, —— London,

CHAPPUIS, (or Chappuy,) AUGUSTINE, about 1710.

CHARLES, THERESS, London.

CHEROTTE, —— Mirecourt, 18th Century.

CHEVRIER, —— Paris, 18th Century.

CHRISTA, JOSEPH PAUL, Munich, 1730.

CHRISTOPHORI, BARTOLOMEO, Florence, 18th Century.

CIRCAPA, THOMASO. Naples, 1730.

CLARK, ——— London.

COLE, THOMAS, London. Forster says no instrument has been preserved of this maker, but that is a mistake. There is in the neighborhood of Sheffield, a very large Tenor with a fine deep tone and the following curious label.

> Made 1690, by
> THOMAS COLE of
> London, on Holborn Hill, who selleth all sorts of Musical Instruments.

COLLINGWOOD, JOSEPH, London, 18th Century.

CORSBY, GEORGE, believed to be formerly a maker at Northampton, and now and for a long time a dealer in Violins, &c., in Princes' Street, Soho, London.

CONWAY, WILLIAM, 1745

COLLIER, SAMUEL, 1755.

CRASK, GEORGE, of various places, has made many Violins in imitation of the Cremona Makers, some of which have been sold by unscrupulous dealers as genuine instruments, an example of which we have seen which was purchased by a professional man, since dead, of a Violinist then on a Musical Tour. It is only right here to say that we believe Mr. Crask to be entirely free from blame in this matter, as he sells these instruments as his own productions.

CROWTHER, JOHN, 1755 to 1810.

CROSS, NATHANIEL, London, about 1720. He was partner at one time with Barak Norman and used his monogram sometimes. He also stamped a Cross in the inside of his instruments as well as used it in his labels. He made some good Violins, which resemble those of Steiner. His mark in the inside of the back is here given.

+

N. C.

A violin of this make which we have seen, has the great fault of having the bass bar cut out of the solid, instead of being glued in, thus contravening the established principles of the art.

CONTRERAS, JOSEPH, Madrid, 1746. An excellent maker, who was particularly celebrated for his copies of Stradiuarius.

D.

DARDELLI, PIETRO, Mantua, about 1500. Made good rebecs, violas and viols da gamba. Fetis mentions some of them as still existing.

DECOMBRE, AMBROISE, Tournay, 1700. to 1735, was said to be one of the pupils of Stradiuarius and made some good instruments of his pattern.

DESPONS, ANTOINE, Paris,—one of the good French Makers, about 1725.

DICKENSON, EDWARD, 1754.

DICKSON, JOHN, Cambridge, 1779

DIEHL, NICHOLAUS, Darmstadt, 17th Century.

DITTON,———London, about 1720.

DODD, THOMAS, Son of Edward Dodd of Sheffield, and who died in London in 1810, at the great age of 105 years (see Bow Makers). Thomas Dodd's instruments have had considerable reputation, but it is believed he was not a maker himself, but employed Bernard Fendt and John Lott, through whose excellent workmanship his name, which he put on the labels, became well known.

DODD, THOMAS. Son of the above; he was drowned in 1843.

DOMINISCELLI—-Ferrara, 18th. Century. A good workman.

DUKE, RICHARD, London, 1767 to 1777. This Artist was very celebrated in his day and his instruments commanded very good prices. He frequently stamped his name on the back, but as far as we have seen, only on inferior productions. Very good instruments may now occasionally be met with at low prices in consequence of the great prejudice in favour of the Italian and other foreign makers.

DURFEL,——Altenburg, made good double Basses. His violins are also said by one authority to be excellent in point of tone.

DUIFFOPRUGCAR, GASPARD, born in the Tyrol, established in Bologna in 1510, and went to Paris at the invitation of Francis 1st.

He afterwards removed to Lyons. This appears to be the first maker of the genuine Violin we have on record, and some instruments still exist to attest the excellence to which he had reached. M. Vuillaume, possesses a Bass Viol, and other Parisian Collectors possess instruments by this ancient artiste.

E.

EBERLE, JEAN ULRIC, Prague, 1719.
Otto says this is one of the most celebrated German Makers and his instruments have been frequently taken by experienced connoisseurs for Italian; the difference being that they "have a sharper or rather not so round and full a tone." Connoisseurs could not be very experienced at that time, if they could mistake for Cremonese, instruments possessing this characteristic, which is exactly what distinguishes the inferior instruments from the genuine.

EBERTI, TOMMASO, about 1730.
EDLINGER, THOMAS, Prague 1715.

EDLINGER, JOSEPH JOACHIM, Pragne, son of Thomas. Visited Italy, and afterwards built some excellent instruments; died in 1748.

ERNST, FRANCOIS ANTOINE, born in Bohemia in 1745. This artiste made some excellent instruments which are said almost to reach the Cremonas in tone. He was also the Author of a Treatise on Instruments. The celebrated Violinist Spohr, author of " the Violin School," is said to have at one time used one of this maker's instruments.

EVANS, RICHARD London, 1742.

F.

FARINATO, PAUL, Venezia, about 1700.

FENDT, or FINTH, Paris, 1763—80. Made good instruments after the Stradiuarius model, some of which followed his style so carefully as to have been taken for those of that master.

FENDT, BERNHARD, born 1775 died 1825. Nephew of the above. He worked first for

Dodd and afterwards for old John Betts. He was a capital workman and made many fine imitations of the Cremonese instruments.

FENDT, BERNARD SIMON, Son of the above, born 1800 died 1852. became partner with Purdy in the well known firm of Purdy and Fendt.

FENDT, MARTIN, brother of the above, born 1812, died 1845.

FENDT, JACOB, born 1815, died 1849.

FENDT, FRANCIS,

FENDT, WILLIAM, Son of Bernard Simon, born 1833, died 1852.

All the Fendts have the reputation of being excellent workmen.

FICHTOLD, HANS, 1612, is said to have made good instruments.

FICKER, JOHANN CHRISTIAN, Cremona 1722.

FICKER, JOHANN GOTLIEB, Cremona 1788.

FLEURY, BENOIST, Paris, about 1720.

FLORENTUS, FLORINUS, Bologna, 1690. Followed the Amati patterns, and has a good reputation in that style.

FORSTER, WILLIAM. The first Violin maker of this now celebrated name, born 1713, died 1801.

FORSTER, WILLIAM, born 1739, died 1808. This maker was very celebrated for his Violas and Violoncellos. He appears to have followed the Steiner pattern in 1762, and the Amati pattern in 1772. His common instruments were not purfled, second class purfled but still much inferior to the third class, " in which," says an authority, " everything was embodied to conduce to excellence and beautiful appearance and to the finest tone;" and again, " his instruments are second to none in merit and the best Europe has ever known, especially his amber coloured Violoncellos, which are renowned for mellowness, volume, and power of tone, equalled by few, surpassed by none." We need scarcely say that this opinion is rather strongly expressed, and may be considered partial. Without at all detracting from the real excellence of Wm. Forster's instruments, which is very great, we may confidently assert that the great

Cremona Makers have had no rivals. Whether in power, purity, and sweetness of tone—or beauty of wood and workmanship—the best instruments of Nicholas Amati, Antonius Stradiuarius, and Joseph Guarnerius have never yet been equalled. Wm. Foster's Violoncellos have, however, (in England at any rate,) been held in high esteem both by players and amateurs, and have realised good prices.

FORSTER, WILLIAM, the third of the name born 1764, died 1824, known as young Forster. His instruments are not so good as those of his father, but still excellent productions.

FORSTER, WILLIAM, the fourth of the name, born 1788, died 1824. A good workman, but not equal to the second William Forster

FORSTER, SIMON ANDREW, son of the above, born 1801, author, in conjunction with William Sandys, F.S.A., of a most elaborate and excellent work from which these particulars are taken, entitled "History of the Violin and other Instruments played on with the Bow, from the remotest times to the present." He is also like the rest of the family, a maker and bears a good reputation.

FORSTER.—Of this noted family Dubourg in his amusing and interesting book, "The Violin," speaks in complimentary terms. He says, "The Forsters, old and young, grandfather and grandson, have, in their department of art, a name that lives."

FOURRIER, NICHOLAS, born at Mirecourt. Settled in Paris, died 1816; good maker, after the Cremona school.

FRITZCHE, SAMUEL, Leipsic, 1787, pupil of Hunger, and made similar instruments. They are of the Italian model and have amber varnish.

FRITZ, BERTHOLD, Leipsic, 1757.

FRANKLAND, —— London, 1785.

FREY, HANS, Nuremberg, lute maker, 15th Century.

FURBER, DAVID, about 1700.

FURBER, MATTHEW, son of David, 1710.

FURBER, JOHN, grandson of David, 1759.

FURBER, MATTHEW, son of the above, died 1840.

FURBER, JOHN, son of Matthew, 1840.

G.

GABRIELLE, GIOVANNI, BAPTISTA, Florence, 18th. Century. considered to be a good Maker.

GAGLIANO, or GALIANO, ALESSANDRO, Naples, about 1710, is generally reckoned as one of the pupils of Stradiuarius, but was more probably only one of his imitators. He made some good instruments of the Stradiuarius model, which possess a bright and sparkling tone; they are, however, generally characterised by less power of tone, Stradiuarius having in this particular the advantage over nearly all his imitators, some of his personal pupils being perhaps the only exceptions.

NOTE.—M. Fetis commences the line of the Gaglianos with Nicolo, 1700, ten years earlier than Alessandro, whom he also calls Gennaro, and ranks him as a maker formed under one of the immediate pupils of Stradiuarius.

GAGLIANO, JANUARIUS, Naples, 1740. Son of Alessandro.

GAGLIANO, NICHOLAUS, Naples. Another son of Alessandro.

GAGLIANO, FERDINANDO, Naples, made to 1790.

GAGLIANO, GUISEPPF, Naples, 1790.

GAGLIANO, GIOVANNI, Naples.

GAGLIANO, ANTONIO, Naples.

GAGLIANO, RAPHAEL, Naples, son of Giovanni.

GAGLIANO, ANTONIO, Naples, son of Giovanni.

GAGLIANO FAMILY.

Most of the instruments made by the Gagliano family possess a good quality of tone, and Amateurs who have no necessity for that great power which Stradiuarius and Guarnerius conferred on their best productions, will do well to secure any genuine Gagliano which they may meet with, rather than risk the chance of getting less merit, under a more pretentious name.

GALERZENA, —— Piedmont, 1790

GAND. —— Paris. A first-rate maker. He was son-in-law to Lupot.

GARANA, MICHAEL ANGELO, Bologna. An excellent maker, about 1700, considered by Fetis to be a pupil of one of those celebrated makers formed in the Cremona schools.

GATTANANI, —— Piedmont, 1790.

GAVINIES, —— Paris, 18th Century.

GEDLER, JOHANN ANTONY, Fissen, Bavaria, 18th Century.

GEDLER, JOHANN BENEDICT, same place and same date.

GERANS, PAUL, Cremona, about 1615.

GERLE, JEAN, Nuremberg, about 1540. Made Lutes, Viols da Gamba, &c.

GILKES, SAMUEL, London, 1787 to 1827. Pupil of the Second William Forster. An excellent maker. His work was most highly finished and his varnish of a rich quality.

GILKES, WILLIAM, born 1811. Not equal as a maker to Samuel.

GIORDANE, ALBERTO, Cremona, 1735.

GOBETTI, FRANCISCO, Venezia, about 1700. A pupil of Stradiuarius, and an excellent artiste.

GOFILLER, MATTEO, Venezia, about 1725. A good maker after Cremona patterns.

GOFILLER, FRANCISCO, Venezia. Brother to Matteo, similar, same date.

GRAGNARIUS, ANTONIO, early part of 18th Century.

GRANCINO, GIOVANNI, Milan, middle of 17th Century.

GRANCINO, PAOLO, do. do.

GRANCINO, GIOVANNI BAPTISTA, Milan, son of first named.

GRANCINO, GIOVANNI BAPTISTA, Milan, early in 18th Century.

GRANCINO, FRANCISCO, son of Giovanni Baptista. This artiste made to about 1760, or rather later.

GRANCINO FAMILY.

These makers produced some very good but not handsome instruments. Lindley is said to have had a Violoncello by one of the Granciuos, the tone of which was very fine and powerful, with light yellow varnish darkened by age; the wood of back and sides very plain, but the belly very fine.

GROBITZ, —— Warsaw, about 1750.
Made some good instruments of the Steiner model.

GUERSAN, —— Paris. An excellent maker, small model, careful finish, and fine tone; about 1730.

GUGEMMOS, —— Fissen, Bavaria.

GUIDANTUS, GIOVANNI FLORENUS, Bologna, about 1750. An excellent maker.

GULETTO, NICHOLAS, Cremona, about 1790.

GUADAGNINI, LORENZO, Cremona, 1690 to 1720. Pupil of Straduarius and highly esteemed as a maker. Followed the style of his celebrated teacher.

Guadagnini is one of the makers especially recommended by Spohr when one of the three great masters cannot be procured. A good specimen of his work will always command a good price.

GUADAGNINI, LORENZO. Placentia and Milan, 1742 Made instruments generally of the smaller model. Was a careful workman and finished his instruments well, and used good varnish.

GUADAGNINI, BAPTISTA. Same places and about same dates, and made similar instruments.

GUADAGNINI, GUISEPPE, Turin, 1751.

GUADAGNINI, GUISEPPE, Parma, 1793.

GUARNERIUS FAMILY.
A more extended account of these great masters will be found in a separate chapter.

GUARNERIUS, ANDREAS, Cremona, born 1630, dates to 1680. Pupil of Hieronymus Amati.

GUARNERIUS, GUISEPPE, son of Andreas, Cremona, dates from 1690 to 1730.

GUARNERIUS, PIETRO, another son of Andreas. Removed in the latter part of his life from Cremona to Mantua.

GUARNERIUS, JOSEPH, nephew of Andreas. Known as Joseph to distinguish him from his cousin of the same name, but who is generally known as Guiseppe.

Joseph was the great maker of the family, born 1683, died 1745, at Cremona.

H.

HARBOUR, —— London, 1785.

HARDIE, MATTHEW, Edinburgh, about 1820. Made some good instruments which occasionly possessed great power, but not always very neat finish.

HARDIE, THOMAS, Son of Matthew, Edinburgh, was also a good workman—died in 1856, from accidentally falling down stairs.

HARE, JOSEPH, London, 1720, is said to have been the first in England to introduce the flat model, all the makers before him and for some time after, following the elevated model of Steiner. He also introduced a varnish of greater transparency than was generally used at that time in England.

HARRIS, CHARLES, London, about 1815.

HARRIS, CHARLES, Son of the above.

HART, JOHN, of Princes Street, Leicester Square, London, pupil of Samuel Gilkes, is a maker; and restorer of instruments, in which latter capacity we have pleasure in stating him to be worthy of the extensive reputation he has acquired. He is also a great connoisseur in old instruments, and has the honour of having formed most of the fine collections in this country. The largest price ever given for a Violin was for one imported by him and which from its beauty, model, varnish and perfection of condition is known by the name of the King Joseph Guarnerius. This instrument is considered quite unique and was sold for 700 guineas. The celebrated collection of Charles Plowden, Esq., which embraces four fine instruments of Stradiuarius and four of Joseph Guarnerius, and which is acknowledged to be the finest collection in the world, was also formed by Mr. Hart. Mr. Plowden's taste being highly cultivated, he rejects any instrument which is not of the very highest order, and therefore it reflects great credit on Mr. Hart's judgment to have succeeded in placing so many fine instruments in the collection of so critical a connoisseur We shall have oc-

casion to mention other celebrated in-
instruments in the Chapters on the Great
Masters of the Art.

HASSERT, —— Rudolstadt, 18th Century.
Made instruments of a high model, which
though he used good wood and finished
them carefully, did not possess very good
tone Very few makers have succeded in
imparting superior tone to high built instruments.

HASSERT, ——, Eisenach, 18th Century,
brother of the above—adopted a different
system, and followed the flatter model of
the Cremona School with considerable success. His instruments are remarkable for
beautiful wood, and Otto speaks very higly
of them, saying that many of them can
only be distinguished from the genuine
Italians by experienced judges. In the
present day we think Otto was partial to
his own countrymen's work, and that there
are very few German instruments which
can be taken for Italian by judges.

HEESOM, EDWARD. London, 1750.

HELMER, CHARLES, Prague, 1740.
 This artiste was a pupil of Eberle, and is considered a careful workman, but used too light a bass bar, which, unless a stronger one be substituted, depreciates the character of his instruments.

HILDEBRANT, MICHAEL CHRISTOPHER, Hamburg. 1765. Esteemed as a good maker.

HILL, WILLIAM, London, 1740. Made some good instruments, but they are said to be deficient in quality in consequence of being built on a wrong principle, the centres having too little wood.

HILL, JOSEPH, London, 1770, brother of the above. Reckoned a superior maker to his brother, and produced some very excellent Violoncellos which obtained him a good reputation, and caused him to be classed high among English makers, but like the others, he is now depreciated in value below his real merits.

HIRCUTT, —— English maker, about 1600.

HOFFMAN, MARTIN, Leipsic, is said to be chiefly known as a skilful lute maker. His

Tenors are considered good, and Otto says his violins have an excellent quality of tone when unspoiled, but are not esteemed on account of their ungraceful appearance.

HOLLOWAY, J., London, 1794.

HORIL, —— (Italian) about 1720.

HULLER, AUGUSTINE, Shœneck, 1775.

HUME, RICHARD, Edinburgh. An early English lute maker; about 1530.

HUNGER, CHRISTOPHER FREDERICK Leipsic, 1787. A good maker who followed the Italian style, used good wood and amber varnish. This maker is classed among the superior German artistes, and his instruments are said to be beautiful.

J.

JACOBS, —— Amsterdam, 18th. Century. This maker imitated the Amatis and produced some good instruments after their Models which also partook of their sweet tone but had little power. One authority we have consulted calls this maker a pupil of Amati, and states that he used whalebone purfling.

JAYE, HENRY, London, 1615. Of this maker we have not been able to find any account unless it be to him that Mace (1676,) refers when he says, speaking of the makers of Viols, " Of such there are no better in the world, than those of Aldred,- Jay, Smith " &c. He was certainly an excellent maker judging from an instrument we have seen which has been converted into a small Violoncello with four strings. It is handsomely finished, with ornamental purfling and good varnish and a well carved head. As a small violoncello the tone is also very good. Dated "in Southwarke," 1615.

JAY, THOMAS, London, about 1700.

JAY, HENRY, London, 1750. It appears that this artiste was best known as a maker of Kits, which were very well made and for which he obtained the extraordinary price in those days of five pounds each. When we remember that four pounds was the price that Stradiuarius got for his best violins in his life time, and from an anecdote told by Mr. Forster, that Cervetto could not even get that price for some he got direct from the maker, we see one of those extraordinary freaks of fashion for which, to use the expression of my Lord Dundreary, no fellow can account

JAUCH, —— Dresden, about 1765, is said to have made good instruments on Cremona models, and is generally placed among the good German makers.

JOHNSON, JOHN, London, 1753.

JULIANO, FRANCISCO. Rome, 1700.

K.

KAMBL, JOHANN, CORNELIUS, 1635.

KENNEDY, ALEXANDER, London, died 1785, and considered to be about 90 years of age This artiste obtained considerable reputation for good and neat work. He followed the Steiner model, and used yellow varnish. It is not known that he made any other instruments than violins.

KENNEDY, JOHN, London, died in 1816, and, considered to be 86 years of age. Made violins and tenors of the Steiner model.

KENNEDY, THOMAS, son of John, London, bears the reputation of a good and neat artiste, and is said to have made at least 300 violoncellos and other instruments in proportion.

KERLIN, JOAN, Brescia, about 1450. This artiste is believed by some inquirers to be the earliest maker of the violin proper, but Fetis says that the only instrument of his that is known, and which was in the possession of Koliker of Paris, and dated 1449, was not really a violin, but a viol with changed neck and mounted with four strings. It would appear, therefore, that the merit of the actual introduction of the real violin belongs properly to Gaspar di Salo.

KIAPOSSE, SAWES, Petersburg, 1718.

KLOTZ, MATTHIAS, Tyrolese, about 1675, considered by Fetis to have been a pupil of Steiner, and the first violin maker of this well known name. He made some instruments, which established his reputation as a careful artiste.

KLOTZ, EGITIA. This maker, who appears
to have been a son of Matthias, is often
considered to be the best maker of this
Family. He is commonly called the pupil
of Steiner, but that must be doubtful.
More probably he followed the Steiner
traditions as exemplified by his father. He
used amber varnish, good wood, and his
instruments are well made and have his
own name upon them.

KLOTZ, GEORGE, brother of Egitia.

KLOTZ, SEBASTIAN, another brother.
We believe this artiste to be the best maker
of the Klotz family. He built large sized
violins, which possess a fine tone and have
excellent varnish.

KLOTZ, MICHAEL,—1771.

KLOTZ, JOSEPH, son of Egitia, Mittenwald an der Iser, 1774. Otto says this
artiste built after his father's system—but
was better acquainted with the qualities of
wood, and his instruments are therefore
superior in tone, but are badly varnished
in their original state.

THE KLOTZ FAMILY.

Spohr enumerates Klotz among the makers whose instruments are worthy of attention, but does not indicate which of them in particular. We have before expressed our opinion that Sebastian ranks highest in merit, which is corroborated by the most experienced connoisseur of the present day. Some violins of this name have achieved a high reputation. Parkes, in his " Musical Memoirs," mentions a Klotz Violin belonging to Mr. Hay, the Leader of the King's Band, for which a Noble Lord offered £300 and an annuity of £100. This seems a most extraordinary offer, for any instrument, unless it were a very fine Stradiuarius or Guarnerius.

KOHL, JEAN, Munich, Luthier to the Court, about 1570. Fetis states that from some old accounts he finds he was paid two florins for a lute, a strange discrepancy in value from the statement of Mace a century later.—(See Bolles.)

KOLDITZ, MATTHIAS JOHANN, Munich, 1722.

KOLDITZ, JAQUES, Rumbourg, in Bohemia, 1790; said to be very good.

KOLIKER, —— Paris, a noted maker and collector, about 1750.

KNITTING, PHILIP, Mittenwald, 1760.

KNITL, JOSEPH, Mittenwald, 1790.

KRINER, JOSEPH, Mittenwald, 1785.

L.

LACASSO, ANTONIO MARIA, Milan, probably the same as Lausa.

LAGETTO, Paris, about 1650. Followed the Amati patterns.

LAMBERT, JOHANN HENRY, Berlin, 1760.

LAMBERT, —— Nancy, 1760. A prolific but not very careful maker, which gained him the name of the Lute Carpenter.

LANDOLPHI, CARLO, Florence, 1750. An excellent maker, who followed the Cremona patterns with considerable success.

LANDOLPHI, FERDINAND, Milan, about same date.

There appears to be some doubt whether there was more than one Landolphi, his name being Carlo Ferdinand, but being mentioned as of both Florence and Milan, and the Christian names given separately, there may have been two. Fetis only mentions Carlo, and locates him at Milan.

LAUSA, ANTONIO MARIA, 1675. A capital imitator of Magini and Gaspar di Salo's instruments, but is said not to have succeeded in rivalling them in tone.

LAUTTEN, L. W. No particulars of this maker; but we find a violin by him in a Catalogue, described as "fine and handsome."

LECLERC, —— Paris, 18th Century

LENTZ, JOHANN NICHOLAUS, London, about 1800. Considered a good workman.

LEWIS, EDWARD. London, about 1700. An excellent maker, used good wood, fine varnish, chiefly of a yellow colour, and was notable for his excellent finish.

LINELLI, or LINAROLLA, —— Venezia, about 1520. A maker of rebecs, viols, and viols da gamba.

LOTT, JOHN FREDERICK, London, born 1775, died 1853. An excellent workman, who made many instruments for Thomas Dodd. He is also very generally known as a first-rate double bass maker.

LOTT, GEORGE FREDERICK, son of the above, was also an excellent workman, and is said to have been chiefly employed by dealers.

LOTZ, THEODORE, Prestburg, about 1785, has a good reputation as a maker of violins.

LUPOT, FRANCOIS, Stuttgard, about 1770.

LUPOT, NICHOLAS, son of Francois, born at Stuttgard, 1758; went to Orleans, 1786, and Paris, 1794; died 1824. This artiste deserves the title of the King of the French makers. He followed the model of Stradiuarius, used excellent wood and good varnish, much in the style of that master. His violins are very fine in tone and resemble the Italian more than any other maker's.

Tolbecque, the violinist has two very fine specimens. His instruments have been frequently selected by the French Conservatoire as prizes for their pupils. They now fetch high prices. Dubourg calls him " a studious artist, whose instruments are in request when a good Cremona is unattainable." He also says, " sixty guineas have been refused for one of his best violins." Spohr in his " Violin School," also recommends his instruments. This artiste published a work on the construction of violins, called " La Chelonomie, ou le parfait Luthier."

M.

MAGGINI, GIOVANNI PAOLO, Brescia, 1590 to 1640. This celebrated artiste was a pupil of Gaspar di Salo. His instruments are highly esteemed, and are both rare and valuable. They are generally of a large pattern, with elevated model, reaching almost to the edges; narrow ribs, double purfling, frequently ending on the top and bottom of the back with an ornament in the shape of a leaf—and fine yellowish brown or golden coloured varnish, of good quality. Some few are said to have deep brown varnish. They possess a tone of a peculiar character—deep, solemn, and somewhat plaintive. Dubourg describes it as " less soft than that of a Stradiuarius, and less potent than a Guarnerius, approaching that of a viol, and has in it a touch of melancholy." From their size these instruments had not been in great favour with violinists until the celebrated De Beriot introduced one, which from its splendid tone brought them at once into esteem, and for which he has been offered almost fabulous sums.

MAGGINI, PIETRO SANTO, Brescia, son of Giovanni Paolo, 1630 to 1680. Followed the same style as his father, but was more particularly famous for his double basses, which the Italians consider to be the best ever made, after those of Gaspar di Salo.

MAIER, ANDREA FERDINAND, Salzburg, 1746. Little is known of this maker except that he made the small instrument on which the immortal Mozart first learned to play the violin, which event, could he have foreseen, would no doubt have compensated him for the want of more general fame.

MALDONNER, —— Bavaria, about 1760.

MALLER, LAUX, Venice. This artiste was an early and highly esteemed maker of lutes. Mace in his curious and very interesting book, " Music's Monument," mentions him as one of the best authors, *i.e.* makers. He also says he has " seen two of his lutes ('pittiful, battered, cracked Things,') valued at £100 apiece." Mace's book was published in 1676. Think of £100 for a lute two hundred years ago, when the value of money was at least six times less than it is now! This would make the comparative value of a " battered" old lute about £600, a sum (with the exception of the King Joseph Guarnerius, mentioned elsewhere) exceeding the highest price we have heard of in modern times. Even the most splendid and perfect violins of Stradiuarius have never realised as much as this "pittiful battered" lute!" In the face of this fact (as we suppose it is) we cannot be surprised that enthusiastic amateurs should in the present day give such large prices for the splendid productions of the great Cremona Makers.

MARIANI, ANTONIO, Pesaro, 1570 to 1620. An imitator of Gaspard di Salo.

MARATTI, —— Verona, 1690. Made good toned violins, but the workmanship has little character.

MARQUIS DE LAIR, —— A French maker about 1800.

MARSHALL, JOHN, London, 1760,

MARTIN, —— London, 1790.

MAUCOTEL, CHARLES, London. An excellent workman, who has produced some beautiful instruments.

MAUSIELL, LEONARD, Nuremburg, 1725. A capital imitator of Steiner, whose style he followed so closely as to render it (as it is stated) difficult to distinguish the one from the other. This is one of the makers praised by Spohr in his "Violin School," as worthy attention when a good Cremona cannot be got.

MAYRHOF, ANDREA FERDINAND, Salzburg, 1740.

MEDARD, HENRY, Paris and Nancy. A French maker, who is generally considered to have been a pupil of Nicholas Amati, and was esteemed nearly equal to his master; but Fetis includes him in his list of the personal pupils of Antonius Stradiuarius.

MERLIN, JOSEPH, London, about 1780. A very ingenious person, who obtained the honour of being mentioned in Madame D'Arblay's " Diary and Letters." His violins were after the Steiner pattern, and well made, but did not approach the Steiner tone.

MEUSIDLER, JEAN, Nuremberg, about 1510. A maker of viols, viols da gamba, &c.

MEZZADIE, ALEXANDER, Ferrara, about 1700. A good maker who followed the Amati style, and is reckoned by Fetis as one of that school.

MIER, —— London, 1786

MILANI, FRANCISCO, Milan, is supposed to be a pupil of Guadagnini and followed his style,—about 1760.

MILLER, —— London, about 1750.

MOHR, PHILIP, Hamburg, 1650.

MONTADE, GREGORIO, Cremona, 1735. Considered to be a pupil of Stradiuarius, but more probably an imitator.

MONTAGNANA, DOMINICO, Venezia, 1725. This excellent artiste made instruments generally of a large size, and used wood of a large and beautiful figure. The varnish exceedingly brilliant and of a rich yellow or yellow red colour, and the tone everything that can be desired. Mr. Perkins had a violoncello of this make, which was originally sold as a Joseph Guarnerius, and was said in the catalogue to be uncommonly fine and handsome. This is another of those careful artistes, whose productions are now in high esteem when one of the three great masters cannot be obtained, and which will very probably hereafter rank with them and become very famous.

MORRISON, JOHN, London, 1780 to 1819.

MORELLA, MORGLATO, Mantua, about 1550. Famous for rebecs, viols, and viols da gamba.

N.

NAMY, —— Paris, about 1800.
NAYLOR, ISAAC, Leeds, 1788.
NEWTON, ISAAC, 1780.
NICHOLAS, —— Geneva, 1790.
NIGGEL, SYMPERTUS, Paris about 1650.
NORMAN, BARAK, London, 1690 to 1740.
 He generally used a monogram formed of the lettes NB. interlaced. This artiste has long been a favourite, and he certainly made some good instruments, which in the present day are depreciated below their real worth, as is the case also with other English makers, whose productions have had to give way before the prevailing preference for Italian instruments. He was partner at one time with Nathaniel Cross, and the instruments then made bear their joint names on the labels.

NORRIS AND BARNES, pupils of Thomas Smith, 1785 to 1818.
NOVELLO, VALENTINO, Venezia, about the middle of 18th Century.

NOVELLO, MARCO ANTONIO, Venezia, same date. Both these makers are in good esteem.

O.

OBUE, BARTOLOMEO, Verona.
ODOARDI, GUISEPPE, early 18th Century.
OTT, JEAN, Nuremberg. Lute maker, 15th Century.
OTTO, JACOB AUGUSTUS, born at Gotha, 1762, died 1830. Author of the celebrated Book on the Construction of the Violin. He made some good instruments which, in his book he says he "proved" by a machine which played them in thirds, fourths, and fifths for a continued period, thus mellowing and perfecting the tone. We do not believe in this doctrine. From all past experience, there can be no doubt that whatever pains or trouble a maker may take to bring his instruments, while new, to bear the character of old, his labour is quite useless. There is no instance of an instrument becoming famous for its fine tone till it had attained a good old age.

Some modern makers use chemical means to mature their violins; but this process is utterly destructive to them, as they become quite rotten through the action of the acid after a lapse of years. Time alone can ripen and mellow all musical instruments made of wood, the violin and the organ especially.

P.

PANORMO, VINCENZIO, born near Palermo, 1734. He appears to have left his native place, and after a temporary sojourn in several towns came to England about 1772, and died in 1813. He was an excellent artiste. His instruments are carefully constructed on Cremona models, and possess a fine tone. He made a few violoncellos which are highly prized, their tone being extremely rich and powerful. They are of the Stradiuarius pattern, mostly of handsome maple for the back and ribs. All his instruments are of a good Italian quality of tone, and are among those which are rising in value as the great masters become rarer and dearer.

PANORMO, JOSEPH, son of Vincenzio, also a good workman.

PANORMO, GEORGE LEWIS, another son of Vincenzio, a celebrated bow maker.

PANORMO, Edward.

PANORMO, GEORGE, probably grandson of Vincenzio.

PAMPHILON, EDWARD, London, 1685. A very clever artiste. Made violins of rather small model, somewhat high built, rich yellow varnish, and sometimes double purfled. The Editor has known one of his instruments, which was in the hands of a rich amateur, in whose house he has heard it played and very much approved.

PANSANI, ANTONIO, Rome, 1785.

PARKER, DANIEL, London, 1714, is considered one of the good old English makers. His instruments have a clear and powerful tone. A first-rate authority calls him an excellent workman; another says though he was otherwise good he used a bad brick red varnish.

PASTA, GAETANO, Brescia, early in 18th Century.

PASTA, DOMINICO, Brescia, same date. Said to have followed the Amati patterns, and deserted the Brescian standard of Gaspar di Salo and Maggini.

PEARCE. JAMES and THOMAS, London, 1780.

PEMBERTON. J., London, 1580. An English maker of considerable talent. Is supposed to have been the maker of the instrument presented by Queen Elizabeth to the Earl of Leicester.

PFRETZSCHNER, GOTTLOB, Cremona, 1749.

PFRETZSCHNER, CARL FREDERICK, Cremona.

PICHOL, —— Paris.

PIQUE, —— Paris. An excellent maker, and the master of Lupot. Spohr recommends Pique's instruments, and Dubourg says they were given as prizes by the French Conservatoire in the beginning of the present Century.

PIERRAY, or PIERRET, CLAUDE, Paris. A charming workman. His violins have been frequently mistaken for Italian by inexperienced judges. They are of a deep red colour and finely finished, with an excellent quality of tone.

PIETE, NOEL, Paris, about 1785, pupil of Saunier. An artiste well spoken of.

PLACK, FRANCIS, Schœnback, 1738. Considered a good maker.

POLLUSHA, ANTONIO, Rome, 1751.

PONS, —— Grenoble, France, 1787. Made large pattern violins with high model, which have no great value.

POSSEN, LAUXMIN, Bavaria, about 1540. Made rebecs, viols, and viols da gamba.

POWELL, ROYAL and THOMAS, London, 1785.

PRESTON, JOHN, York, 1789.

R.

RACCERIS, —— Mantua, 1670, believed to have been a partner with one of the Gaglianos, and made similar instruments.

RAF, —— Bavaria.

RAMBEAUX, —— Paris, a pupil of Gand, and an excellent workman.

RAPHAEL, NELLA, Brescia, 18th Century. This artiste was of the school of Maggini, and his instruments are said to have the scrolls sculptured, and to have inscriptions on the sides.

RAUCH, JAQUES, Mannheim, 1730 to 1740. Considered to be a very good maker.

RAUCH, SEBASTIAN, 1742 to 1763.

RAUCH. —— Breslau.

RAUCH, —— Wurtzburg.

Otto praises the instruments of the two brothers of Breslau and Wurtzburg. He says they are excellent violins but have a shape and model peculiar to themselves and entirely different to the Italian or Steiners, but possess when uninjured a full, round and powerful tone. If Otto had told us what instruments were like instead of what they were not like, his book would have been more valuable.

RAUT, JEAN, Bretagne. He was at Rennes till 1790. Made good instruments after the Guarnerius school.

RAYMAN, JACOB, London, 1641. The instruments of this maker were very highly valued formerly. He is considered one of our best old English artistes.

REICHEL, JOHANN GOTTFRIED, Absom. An imitator of Steiner.

REICHEL, JOHANN CONRAD, Neukirch, 1779.

REISS, —— Bamburg. A capital imitator of Steiner, and made excellent instruments.

REMY, —— Paris.

RENISTO, —— Cremona, 1740, pupil of Carlo, Bergonzi. His instruments are very similar to those of his master, but rather higher modelled, and the workmanship somewhat rougher.

RETANTINO, —— No particulars of this maker.

RIMBOUTS, PETER, Amsterdam.

ROOK, JOSEPH, London, 1777 to 1852. A good workman, who imitated Forster.

ROSS, JOHN, 1562. An early maker of lutes.

ROTH, CHRISTIAN, Augsburg, 1675.

ROVELIN, —— 18th Century.

RUDGER, —— Cremona—not one of the Ruggeri Family. Made some good instruments of the high build, and deep sides, and used fine varnish.

RUGGERI, FRANCISCO, Cremona, 1640 to 1684. This celebrated maker is considered to have been a pupil of Antonius Amati, and made many excellent instruments which bear a high reputation. They rank next to the Amati. Their quality is similar, and the style of work is easily seen to belong to the same class. There are a few violins by this maker of the same pattern as the Grand Amatis, which are said to surpass the latter, having more wood in them, which was detrimental when they were made, but which age has mellowed, and they now possess a strong and free vibration. Many of the Ruggeris have varnish little inferior to that of Stradiuarius and Guarnerius. This artiste ranks highest in the family in the estimation of the connoisseur. His work is extremely clean. The next is Govanni Baptista, rather higher built and sound holes rather broader. The scrolls are larger than those of Amati but of the same type, There are many splendid violoncellos of these makers and a few tenors. Some of the former are very large. Francisco Ruggeri is mentioned by Spohr in his list of instruments to be sought for in the absence of the three great makers, Nicholas Amati, Antonio Stradiuarius and Joseph Guarnerius.

RUGGERI, GUIDO, Cremona, 1679.

RUGGERI, GIOVANNI BAPTISTA, son of Francisco. Brescia, 1696. Mentioned above.

RUGGERI, PIETRO GIACOMO. Brescia 1700 to 1720. The celebrated violoncellist Piatti plays on an instrument by this maker, and the tone is uncommonly fine and sonorous as all who have heard him know.

RUGGERI, VINCENZIO, Cremona, 1700 to 1730.

RUPPERT, FRANCIS, Erfruth, made some excellent instruments of a very flat model, but generally omitted the linings and corner blocks as well as the purfling. They are nevertheless esteemed in Germany. They have a dark brown amber varnish.

S.

SAINT, PAUL, Paris, about 1650. An excellent French maker.

SALO, GASPAR DI, Brescia, dates from 1560 to 1610. This celebrated artiste was the contemporary of the ancient Amatis, and is thought by some connoisseurs to have been the master of Andrew. However that may be, as there can be no certainty of the fact, the varnish on which the great Cremonese makers established that notable reputation which distinguishes them to the present day, bears a strong analogy to that of Gaspar di Salo, however they may have derived it. In this respect, also, Gaspar excells Maggini, his pupil and follower, who was evidently not initiated into the secret of making that excellent varnish which characterises his master.

The pattern of the instruments which the two early and famous chiefs of the

Cremonese and Brescian Schools built, is however totally different. Those of Gaspar are large, massive, double purfled, and with large sound holes. Andrew is noted for a small pattern, and if he studied in the Brescian workshop, he discarded the style he found there (varnish excepted) and aimed at altogether a different object in his own productions. Those of Gaspar di Salo are constructed with capacity and strength to produce a considerable volume of tone. The Cremonese Artiste on the other hand, made instruments which, both in their proportions and adjustment, were especially adapted for the production of a sweet but not powerful tone. Gaspar's instruments seem to foreshadow in their tone and power, those of Stadiuarius and Joseph Guarnerius, while the Amatis seem generally to have been contented with producing a tone of surpassing sweetness. Gaspar also succeded in giving to his productions that fine tone which seems to have been especially aimed at by the early makers, but as he also from the size and strength of his instruments, produced more tone, he may be considered far the superior of Andrew, the first of the Amatis. It is on this account that in the present day, Gaspar di Salo is esteemed as the greatest maker of his time, and connoisseurs value his instruments accordingly.

There are not many violins by this great master, but of tenors and double basses more. These are very fine and rich in tone. He was not however famous for giving so very high a finish to his works as was afterwards attained at Cremona. His violins are described as rather long, and with a gentle elevation from the sides to the centre. The sound holes straight and large, well cut and parallel, and double purfling. The varnish is generally of a rich brown. These are the chief external characteristics, but they have always possessed that "which passeth show," and commanded the esteem of the dilettanti in that rich quality of tone which is the first essential in a perfect instrument.

Signor Dragonetti, the greatest double

bass player of our day, used one of Gaspar's instruments, which was presented to him on account of their admiration of his wonderful talent, by the order of the Convent of St. Mark at Venice. Shortly before his death the Duke of Leinster offered him £700 for it, a princely sum, but it was refused, as Dragonetti did not feel justified in parting with it, and he ordered in his will that it should be returned to the convent at Venice, which was accordingly done. Ole Bull has a very celebrated violin of Gaspar's make. In the first place, it was sculptured with Caryatides, by the great Florentine artist, Benvenuto Cellini, at the special command of another eminent person, Cardinal Aldobrandini, who presented it to the museum of Inspruck in the Tyrol. In 1809 that city was assaulted by the French, the museum was plundered, and this violin carried to Vienna, where it became the property of another notable person, the Councillor Rehazek, who was famous for his collection of ancient musical instruments. He left it by will to another still more celebrated person, Ole Bull, the distinguished Norwegian violinist, by whom it was exhibited in London in 1862, and with whom it still remains. To our description of Gaspar's instruments we should add that his tenors and double basses are of a rather broader form than his violins.

SALLE, —— Paris, 1800. This artiste was an excellent workman, and famous also as a judge of old instruments.

SANONI, GIOVANNI BAPTISTA, Verona.

SANTI, GIOVANNI, Naples, 1730.

SANCTUS SERAPHINO, Venezia, about 1730. An excellent workman, whose instruments possess almost the beautiful finish of Stradiuarius. He used handsome wood of small figure, and his varnish is often beautiful in the extreme. The model however approaches that of the Steiner school, and the tone is therefore generally wanting in fullness and roundness. He made also a few violoncellos with similar characteristics.

SAPINO, —— Cremona. Pupil of Guiseppe Cappa, made instruments after the style of the Amati.

SANZO SANTINO, —— Milan,

SAUNIER, —— born in Lorraine 1740. An excellent artiste whose instruments are reckoned among the best of the French school.

SCHEINLEIN, MATTHIAS FREDERICK, Langenfeld, born 1710, died 1771.

SCHEINLEIN, JEAN MICHAEL, Langenfeld, born 1751. Made instruments which are said to be good but not strongly built.

SCHMIDT, —— Cassel, mentioned by Otto as living in 1817, and praised by him as an excellent maker. His instruments are of the flat model of Stradiuarius, but have the edges larger and the purfling further from the sides.

SCHONGER, FRANCIS, Erfurth, made high modelled instruments, but of poor tone.

SCHONGER, GEORGE, Erfurth, son of the above, modelled his instruments in the

Italian style and produced some very superior examples.

SCHORN, JACOB, Salzbourg.

SCHORN, JOHANN, Inspruck, 1688.

SCHOTT, MARTIN, Prague.

SHAW, —— London, 1656.

SIMPSON, JOHN, London, 1790.

SIMPSON, J. and J., son of the above.

SIMON, —— Salzbourg, 1722.

SIMON, —— Paris.

SMITH, HENRY, London, 1629. This may be a celebrated maker of viols, &c., mentioned by Mace, 1676, as one of the best then known.

SMITH, THOMAS, London, 1756 to 1799. This well known maker was a pupil of Peter Wamsley. His violoncellos are of the Steiner model, and some of them possess considerable power, and were formerly highly esteemed, but they are now considered to be deficient in quality and wanting in the rich fine tone of the Italian artistes. Notwithstanding, they are still favourites in the country; the editor knows two of his violoncellos which have been respectively sold for £30 and £40 within a few years.

SMITH, WILLIAM, London, 1771.

SOLOMON, —— pupil of Bocquay, a good French artiste.

SPEILER, —— 18th Century.

STADELMANS, DANIEL, 1744, Vienna.

STADELMANS, JOHANN JOSEPH, Vienna, 1784. Fame speaks very highly of this maker, who closely imitated Jacob Steiner and ranks next to him among the German makers.

STEINER, JACOB, of Absom in the Tyrol, born about 1620, date of death not known, but at about the age of seventy retired to a Convent.

See separate chapter on this celebrated artiste.

STOSS, FRANCIS, Bavaria.

STORIONI, LORENZO, Cremona, living in 1782, said to be the last of the great Cremona makers. Forster says his instruments resemble those of Joseph Guarnerius, and that Vieuxtemps' solo violin in 1861, was by this master, and was very much admired. His violoncellos are very powerful. The author knows a violin which an authority says is by Storioni, but which the owner considered to be by Antonius and Hieronymus Amati. The same authority says there are only two in England of this make. It possesses a splendid fine full and rich tone, beautiful wood for the belly, but the back rather plain, varnish deep yellow with reddish tinge. Workmanship not very fine. We mention those little known artistes' instruments when we have seen them, because they are now rising in value and are esteemed as likely to afford good instruments to those who cannot afford those of the three great masters.

STRADIUARIUS, ANTONIUS, Cremona, born 1644, died 1737.

See separate chapter for a fuller account of this celebrated artiste.

STRADIUARIUS, HOMOBONO, Cremona, son of Antonius; made instruments under

the direction of his father, which were signed
"*Sub disciplina A. Stradiuarius.*"

STRADIUARIUS, FRANCISCO, Cremona, another son of Antonius, and signed in the same manner as his brother.

STRAUBE, —— Berlin, 1770. Constructed after the Italian model. His instruments are scarce and good.

STRNAD, GASPAR, Prague, 1781 to 1793. This maker bears a good reputation.

STURIONUS, LAURENTIUS. See Storioni.

SURSANO, SPIRITUS, Coni, 1764.

T.

TAYLOR, —— London, 1770 to 1820.

TECHLER, DAVID, first established himself at Salzburg, and afterwards went to Venice, where the story goes that he was so persecuted by other makers that he fled to Rome, about 1706. He made some excellent and beautiful instruments. They have fine yellow varnish and resemble those of the Tyrolean school of Albani and others. Lindley had a violoncello by this maker which was very fine, and powerful in tone. Another was sold a few years ago by auction, for £50. We have seen a violin of this maker, with very beautiful wood and highly finished workmanship, the tone of which was very pure and polished.

TENZEL, ——— One of our catalogues contains a violin by this maker, but we have no particulars.

TEODITI, JEROME, Rome, 1750.

TESTATOR, IL VECCHIO, Milan, about 1520. A claim has been made for this maker that he was the first to give the name of violino to the reduced viol

TERRESIO, ——— An Italian who died in 1853, was a most eminent judge of instruments. His whole existence seemed to be centered in his art, and his eye became so practised that when travelling to discover old instruments, he took them all to pieces, sides, backs, heads, and all parts, forming a conglomerate mass of pieces of valuable violins. The object of so doing was to avoid the customs' dues which are of course heavy on old instruments. When he reached his destination, he would replace them without the aid of a single mark. After his death his house, or rather his hermitage, was visited by connoisseurs, who fond it strewed with different parts of instruments, some being found in the most out of the way places. He had the major part of all the great instruments through his hands. Among other valuable instruments found in his house after his death, was a Gaspar di Salo double bass and a Bergonzi double bass—the latter unique. Both these instruments are now in Mr. Hart's possession. The Gaspar di Salo is very perfect and its tone is unsurpassed. The Bergonzi is quite a curiosity, from its being the only one of his make known. He visited this country during the Exhibition of 1851, and was deeply gratified upon seeing so many high class instruments among the dilettanti here, and the taste and zest the English have in forming collections.

TESTORE, CARLO GUISEPPE, Cremona, about 1700. This artiste made some very good instruments after the Guarnerius pattern. The wood of the backs of his violoncellos is mostly pear tree, and the bellies are of splendid wood. The tone is very powerful, but not always so smooth as might be wished. This is another rising name. The celebrated double bass player Bottesini, uses one of this maker's instruments which possesses a splendid tone, and is sufficient to stamp Testore as an excellent maker. If any of his smaller instruments possess as good and fine a tone as this double bass he must be ranked among the best Italian artistes. Use will probably wear away the want of smoothness at present complained of in some of them.

TESTORE, CARLO ANTONIO, Milan, about 1710 to 1730.

TESTORE, PAOLO ANTONIO, Milan, about 1720 to 1740. Both the above have the reputation of being good makers. Of these artistes we have a note which states that their model was flat, resembling Joseph Guarnerius in shape, but the varnish very inferior and void of colour.

THOROWGOOD HENRY, London, the 18th century.

TOBIN, —— London, 1800 to 1836. This maker cut most beautiful heads, and his work was neatness in the extreme, so much so indeed as to rob it of decided character.

TONINI, FELICE, Bologna.

TONINI, ANTONIO, Bologna.

TONINI, CARLO, Bologna.

TONINI, GUIDO, Bologna.

We have no special information on these makers, but they are generally ranked among the good Italian makers.

TONONI, CARLO, Venezia, 1699

TONONI, GIOVANNI, Venezia, 1699. The instruments by Tononi are worthy of the highest praise. They are however very scarce. They are of the large pattern, and flat model, with good varnish, and everything about them, including a superior tone, to entitle them to be ranked as excellent instruments.

TORING, —— London.

TRUNCO, —— Cremona, 1660.

U.

URQUART, THOMAS, London, 1650. An excellent old English maker. He used beautiful varnish (for English) and made many small violins which are useful to young players, being old and the price reasonable.

V.

VALLER, —— Marseilles, 1683.
VERON, —— Paris, about 1725. Highly esteemed in France.
VIARD, NICHOLAS, Versailles, about 1730.
VIBRECHT, GYSBERT, Amsterdam, 1707.
VIMERCATI, PAULO, Venezia, 1700.
VOGEL, WOLFGANG, Nuremberg.
VUILLAUME, JEAN, 1700 to 1740. Worked with Straduarius, and made some good instruments under his own name.
VUILLAUME, JEAN BAPTISTE, Paris. Now living. Famous for his copies of Cremonese instruments. This artiste obtained by personal researches in Cremona the particulars of the life of Stradinarius, which Fetis has embodied in his book.

W.

WAGNER, JOSEPH, Constance, 1733.

WAMSLEY, PETER, London, 1727. A celebrated artiste, who made many excellent instruments. Those with the dark brown varnish are the most valuable. They were mostly of the Steiner patterns. Mr. J. Rodgers, organist of Doncaster Parish Church, has a very beautiful tenor by this maker, which is built in the shape of a double bass, and with very peculiar sound holes instead of the usual S S.

WEAVER, SAMUEL, London.

WEISS, JACOB, Salzburg, 1761.

WENGER, GREGORIO FERDINAND, Salzburg, 1761.

WEYMANN, CORNELIUS, Amsterdam, 1682.

WIGHTMAN, GEORGE, 1761.

WITHALM, LEOPOLD, Nuremberg, 1765 to 1788. Otto says this maker's instruments are worthy the attention of the virtuoso, and are extremely like those of of Steiner, and difficult to distinguish from them.

WISE, CHRISTOPHER, London, 1656.
WORNUM, —— London, 1794.
WRIGHT, DANIEL, London, 1745.

Y.

YOUNGE, JOHN, London, 1724.

Z.

ZANETTO, PEREGRINO, Brescia, about 1510. A maker of rebecs, violas, and viols da gamba.

ZANTI, ALESSANDRO, Mantua, about 1770. Reckoned among the good Italian makers.

BOW MAKERS.

It will not be considered out of place in the course of a biographical account of the principal makers of violins, to give a short notice of some eminent persons without whose labours, the violin itself would never have been developed as it has been, to wit, violin bow makers. Much of the elegant finish and refinement of tone and style which distinguish the great players of the violin, if not due altogether to the bow, by which the tone is produced, is at all events greatly aided by it. A Paganini will have a Tourte bow, and so will every other great master, if he can get one. There must be something therefore in the bow, as well as in the violin, more than meets the eye of a casual observer. We have not here space to enter into the subtle niceties which distinguish the bows of Tourte of France. of Dodd of England, and others. Suffice it to say that whoever boasts of an excellent violin should match it with a superior bow. One is incomplete without the other. There are many excellent makers, but we must content ourselves with briefly noticing the most prominent. Suffice it to say in the way of advice and warning that whether the amateur buy an old or a new bow, let him see that its flexibility, which is its great merit, is perfect, and that it is still strong though light and straight. Mr. Bishop in his edition of Otto says the finest bows are those of Vuillaume! He does not even mention any others. Tourte and Dodd do not deem to be worthy his remembrance! There must be nevertheless something in the bows of these makers which commands great respect, for any performer of skill will give (if he can get one, that is the difficulty,) ten or twelve times the amount for a perfect Tourte, which will buy a Vuillaume! There is no doubt that Vuillaume manufactures good bows—but to rank them highest is so palpable a misrepresentation that we have thought it necessary to enter a protest against it.

TOURTE, FRANCIS, Paris, born 1747, died 1835. This is conceded, by all the best judges, to be the greatest maker we have ever known, in fact the Stradiuarius of the bow. His father and grandfather were instrumental in improving the bow, but Francis Tourte brought it to the greatest perfection. His bows are light and flexible, yet straight. They are highly finished and made of the finest Brazil wood. He himself sold his bows mounted with gold, at 12 louis, (£11 4s. 6d.) each; with silver $3\frac{1}{2}$ louis (£3 5s. 6d. It is said the reason of his charging so much was that he found so great a difficulty in getting wood fine enough to satisfy his critical judgment, and that he also made no scruple to break any which did not reach his standard of perfection; he was therefore compelled to charge those sums for such as he permitted to go forth. Whoever wishes to match his cherished Cremona with an equally fine bow will get a Tourte if he can.

LUPOT, of Paris, was another excellent maker. His bows are not quite so light as those of Tourte, but they are in all other respects highly esteemed.

DODD, EDWARD, born at Sheffield, and died in London, at the age of 105 years, in 1810, was distinguished as an improver of the bow in England, about the same time that the Tourtes were founding their great reputation in France. The great maker of this name, however, and who has achieved the honourable title of the Tourte of England, is

DODD, JOHN, the son of Edward. The best bows of this maker are highly esteemed, and partake of all the excellencies of those of Tourte. Some of them, however, are rather short, which is perhaps their only defect.

After these come the bows of Panormo, Pecatte, Tubbs, Vuillaume, and other English and Foreign artistes, whose best bows are much esteemed.

As between old and new bows, we would observe that, in general modern bows are nearly as useless as new violins. The wood of which most of them are made is very inferior to that of the older artistes, and there is always a doubt whether they will stand continued use and remain straight and flexible. With an old bow, if it is straight, there is no fear, with ordinary care, of its remaining so. A good bow is as important as a good violin.

THE GREAT CREMONA MAKERS.

THE AMATI FAMILY.

Cremona! Who has not heard of this now celebrated Italian city? And yet but for a fiddle maker it is very probable indeed that it would never have been known beyond the circle of its own local interests and its relations with neighbouring cities. Now, however, its name is a spell to conjure with. A Cremona Violin is, to a rich amateur, a loadstone that is sure to attract the shining metal from the depths of his purse. Seven hundred pounds have been given for a Guarnerius Violin! Think of that ye dilettanti who are so proud of your pictures and marbles! Even the poor fiddler has his Mecca far away, and it is called Cremona.

Like pictures, the Cremona Violins are real works of art, and like them also, were once to be had for trifling sums. Cuyps and Paul Potters, Stradiuarii and Guarnerii were once to be had for three or four pounds each that are now worth as many hundreds. A Cremona instrument has even been considered a worthy gift to pass between crowned heads, Pope Pius V. having presented a violoncello by Andreas Amati to Charles IX. of France. Fleeting however are the honours of time! Cremona has lost its most famous names from among its citizens, and with them its most distinguished characteristic. For nearly a hundred years no maker of great skill has arisen to dispute the glory of the place with the Amati, Stradiuarius, and Guarnerius, by whom the fame of Cremona will be carried to the latest generations.

It is now about three centuries since there flourished at Cremona its first great violin maker. Andreas Amati appears to have been born there in 1520, and died in 1580. The family was an ancient one, and is mentioned as early as 1097 in the records of the city. It is a remarkable fact, and shows in a strong light the difference of manners and customs in different countries that both Amati and Stradiuarius seem to have been of ancient and honourable families, and yet notwithstanding their adopting an avocation which would in England be thought to tarnish an old family name, they lived and died respected and honoured by their fellow citizens. There is no account of how or of whom Andrew Amati acquired the art of violin making; but it is clear that by some means he had attained to a considerable amount of skill. Under the head of Gaspar di Salo, we have however hazarded a conjecture that he had been to Brescia for the first principles of the art, but that he had adopted little that he found there except the varnish and the general routine of the workshop. Some of his instruments are described as beautifully made, and to have amber varnish of excellent quality of a deep rich yellow tinted with brown or light red colour. His violins appear to have been chiefly of the small pattern and high model. The backs are mostly cut the reverse way of the grain to the present rule, forming what are now termed " slab" backs. They possess a delicate graceful tone of wonderful sweetness, which has also been more or less the chief characteristic of the other makers of this family. With reference to this peculiarity, an eminent writer observes that in the times in which the Amati lived, the tone was not required to be of that powerful character which modern players demand, and that such an immense tone as many later instruments possess would not then have been tolerated. This is very probable, and may account also for the elevated model which was adopted both by Andrew and some others of the Amati. This model conjoined with their beautiful workmanship and generally small size, combined to produce that elegant delicious sweet tone which of all other makers, the Amatis especially possess. They also, all of them, made a greater number of instruments of the smaller size than what is known as the grand pattern, no doubt because the tone produced by them was found generally sufficient. They were also made to carry a much lower bridge and a lighter bass bar than are now used, and the proportions

were arranged accordingly. On this point
M. Maugin, author of a Treatise, entitled
Manuel du Luthier, makes some remarks which
we have translated as pertinent and valuable.
Speaking on the subject of repairing old instruments, he says, " There is no violin maker
now, who does not put, whether in the instruments he has to repair, or in those which he
makes, a much stronger bar than those which
were employed by the great makers themselves.
They must have felt the necessity of doing this
or they would not all act in this way. Now
what is the reason of this mode of working? I
have seen in the hands of rich amateurs, several instruments which have been preserved with
a religious care, absolutely in the form which
Amati and Stradinarius had given to them.
The bridges of these violins had only an inch
and a fraction of height above the belly, while
now-adays bridges have a height of an inch
and (say) three-eighths. Now, the belly being
put into vibration by strings at a great distance
from it, and these strings vibrating by themselves more at the distance of fourteen lines
than at twelve, it has been found necessary to

strengthen the bar which, without that, being drawn into too great a vibration, would give to the strings sol and re a cottony sound which would have quite spoiled the goodness of the instrument." M. Maugin does not say why higher bridges are now used, but there is no doubt on this point. All judges concur that the pitch having been so greatly raised since the old instruments were built, a stronger bar has been found necessary, to counterbalance the increased tension of the higher bridge.

Andrew Amati gave to his instruments a still more decided swell than the later members of his family, his successors no doubt finding a diminution in the rise of the model to produce a fuller if not a sweeter tone. This principle was gradually carried forward till it culminated in Antonius Stradiuarius, who brought it to perfection and demonstrated that the flat model produced the greatest vibration and consquently the most powerful tone. Otto in his celebrated work on the Construction of the Violin, does not mention Andrew Amati, but says that those of Hieronymus were the oldest Cremona

Violins. This is one of the mistakes in his original work which renders it comparatively useless. Connoisseurs and collectors have dissipated those errors, and we now know to a certainty that to Andrew Amati of Cremona, and Gaspar di Salo of Brescia, (of whom also Otto was ignorant,) we owe the establishment of these two great schools of violin making. From their great age, the instruments of these two great makers are now very rare. They are most of them about three centuries old, and though they appear to have made a considerable number, they have through the influences of time and accident gradually disappeared. Some of Andrew Amati's instruments are still left however in the hands of dilettanti and collectors, and retain that distinguishing characteristic of delicious and sympathetic quality which has been the chief charm of all the Amati productions. Andrew had a brother called NICHOLAS, of whom little appears to be known.

After ANDREW, as great makers, come his two sons ANTONIUS and HIERONYMUS, who flourished from 1550 to 1634. ANTONIUS made many small pattern violins, which possess in the highest degree the distinguishing characteristic of the family—a sweet but not powerful tone. He also constructed some of a larger pattern. ANTONIUS and HIERONYMUS conjointly built a number of large pattern violins, which are of high finish and beautiful wood. They are very highly esteemed, and a well preserved example will command a large price. NICHOLAS was the greatest artiste of this deservedly celebrated family, and many instruments still exist to attest the excellence of his workmanship and his knowledge of the proportions requisite to produce a fine tone. He also built many small pattern instruments, but he appears to have almost anticipated Stradinarius and succeeded in producing some instruments of the grand pattern which possess a very powerful as well as sweet tone, and are considered to rival in every respect the famous instruments of that great master. Some of his violins possess a distinguishing mark in a rather abrupt rise in the centre. Otto describes it as a "sharp ridge." It is not exactly so, but is still very different to the gradual swell on the other Cremona instruments.

His best violins, which are known by the title of Grand Amatis, are those which approximate closely to the very best instruments of Stradiuarius and Guarnerius. There can be no doubt therefore, that in these fine specimens of his skill, he had hit upon the same principles which afterwards guided those distinguished artistes in the construction of those most renowned violins which now command the admiration of violinists throughout the world.

We have said that the chief characteristic of the Amati violins is a sweet but not powerful tone. It is necessary to qualify and explain this remark. From their excellent construction and beautiful wood, which has evidently been selected with the greatest care for its resonant quality—their age and long and careful use, their tone is divested of all extraneous properties, and become fine and pure. Notwithstanding therefore their original small tone, when fitted with the modern appliances of larger bars and higher bridges, some have been found quite competent for all purposes. In 1861 the celebrated instrument by Antonius Amati, which was presented by George IV. to

o

Francois Cramer, was sold by auction, and it was stated in the catalogue that that great performer always led the Ancient and other concerts on that instrument. The fact no doubt is that it is the fine and pure quality of tone that tells, arising from age, constant use, and beautiful woods. They seem to be now divested of all extraneous characteristics and are become refined and ethereal, and are in fact the nightingales of the stringed tribe. That the Stradiuarius and Guarnerius have equal quality combined with more power arising from their flatter model is undoubted, and therefore they are the most valued. It is believed that the finest specimen of the skill of Nicholas Amati is in the possession of Ole Bull. It is of the large pattern, and possesses a magnificent tone, as many of our readers have no doubt heard.

We think we shall please our readers by inserting verbatim the following excellent description of the Amati instruments, furnished to us by an able and experienced connoisseur. He says :—

"NICHOLAS AMATI and the BROTHERS AMATI. The tone is with few exceptions sweet in quality and seldom powerful, but admirably suited to the amateur. The workmanship is of the highest order, which conduces to this result. The wood must have been selected with great judgment. The bellies are nearly always of a fine reedy nature. Sometimes the backs are whole backs (in one piece), at others in two, more often the latter. The varnish of a beautiful amber colour, and there are a few instances of fine red. The sides generally rather shallow, heads of exquisite form and well defined. The care bestowed upon them alone bespeaks the hand of the artist. There are several magnificent tenors and violoncellos, and perhaps three or four double basses. The tenors are sometimes seen of large size. The Amati family made several sets of instruments for foreign courts, which bear their particular arms, mostly beautifully painted on the backs. The violins known as Grand Amatis are the best, and were made by Nicholas Amati. They take their name from their size. He also made many long pattern instruments, and also several three quarter violins, which have conferred a great boon upon juvenile violinists who are able to purchase them, by giving them an opportunity of early becoming familiar with the irreproachable Italian quality of tone."

In reference to the remark made in the preceding paragraph, it is recorded that a set of instruments, no doubt one of those therein alluded to, was made for Charles 9th of France by Andrew Amati, consisting of twenty-four violins, six violas, and eight basses. These were lost from Versailles in 1790, and have not been recovered, except two which M. Cartier discovered some years since. Notwithstanding that Andrew Amati was the first maker of any note, except Gaspar di Salo of Brescia, it is clear that he had attained an astonishing amount of skill, as there is an account of a violoncello which was offered by auction at the sale of the celebrated Sir Wm. Curtis's instruments by Mr. Musgrave, who in the catalogue stated that "a document was given to the proprietor when he purchased this instrument, stating that it was presented by Pope Pius 5th to Charles 9th of France for

his chapel. It has been richly painted, the arms of France being on the back, and the motto 'Pietate et Justitia' on the sides. The tone of this violoncello is of extraordinary power and richness." Mr. Forster supposes this to have been one of the instruments mentioned before, but that would destroy the value of the document given to Sir William, because if Andrew Amati made it for Pope Pius 5th, who presented it to Charles 9th it could not have been one of those made by him expressly for that monarch. It is clear however that the tone was both grand and fine, and therefore the first of the Amatis must have attained great ability in his art. We have before mentioned the celebrated Nicholas Amati violin, dated 1679, formerly the property of the same distinguished collector, Sir W. Curtis, and which has since been sold by Mr. Hart to the great violinist Ole Bull. This is considered the finest specimen of the Amati skill and was thus described in the catalogue of the sale—
"This is justly considered as one of the most beautiful and finest instruments in the WHOLE WORLD." The Count de Castelbarco of Milan,

possessed a quartett of instruments by Nicholas Amati, which have since been sold in London (see the article on Stradiuarius.) M. Fetis describes these as *admirable,* but as our readers will see, the English connoisseurs do not appear to have coincided generally with the critic on their quality, as only one of them produced any great price. There is a splendid grand Amati in the hands of an amateur in Derbyshire, which formerly belonged to Mr. Hankey the banker, for whom it was purchased with others by Viotti, who dedicated several of his compositions to him. This instrument possesses in an eminent degree the admirable qualities of the Amati tone, with also considerable power. Another of the same set in the same hands is a splendid Stradiuarius of the large pattern with a magnificent tone. There are many fine examples of the different makers of this celebrated name in this country. English connoisseurs suffer those of no other nation to excel them in their collections.

ANTONIUS STRADIUARIUS.

A most interesting account of Antonius Stradiuarius, who is generally thought to be the greatest maker of the violin—has been published by M. Fetis, and translated into English by Mr. Bishop of Cheltenham. In addition to records of his family, which was an ancient one in Cremona, obtained by M. Vuillaume in his persevering labours in search of information, and which he placed at the service of M. Fetis—the latter enters deeply into what we may call the science of violin making, and presents us with many interesting and valuable experiments which have been made on fragments of the great instruments, in order to ascertain the exact principles which enabled Stradinarius to build with such undeviating and brilliant success. The book is well worthy the perusal of all amateurs of the violin.

ANTONIUS STRADIUARIUS.

Antonius Stradiuarius was born in Cremona, in 1644, and died there in 1737, having lived in the peaceful exercise of his art to the great age of ninty-three. There is a violin still extant which bears his signature and proves this fact. In the early part of his life, he was a pupil of Nicholas Amati, and some of his early productions bear his master's name, as seems to have been the custom. These instruments have the Amati characteristics, and have some of the backs cut the contrary way of the grain, forming what are known by the name of "slab" backs. He afterwards enlarged his model and adopted a flatter pattern, and arrived at the greatest perfection about 1700. From that period to 1725, everything he made bore the impress of the great master. In shape, the cutting of the S holes, the varnish, and the accuracy with which all the parts were adjusted in harmonical relation, from that time he excelled all who had gone before him, or who have since attempted the difficult task of vieing with him. All these instruments are of the flat pattern, which is now proved to be best adapted for the production of a rich, deep and powerful tone. It would appear that the more elevated model used before his time, although it allowed of very fine quality of tone, tended to prevent that strong vibration which is the cause of great tone. M. Fetis insists that the violins of Stradiuarius were as good and fine in quality of tone when made as they are now, contrary to the established opinion that time is necessary as well as use for refining and perfecting all violins. He gives an instance of a violin made by Stradiuarius, now in Paris, which he states has never been played upon—but we must beg to doubt this fact. Though we are ready to admit that the careful adjustment of the different parts and the selection of fine wood, would tend to perfect the tone of these instruments, much sooner than others less carefully fashioned, yet in the instance he brings forward in support of his theory, it does not appear quite so clear that the violin never had been played upon. On the contrary, there are many years unaccounted for, in his description of it, during which it might have undergone considerable use. It appears almost impossible that while in the hands of various possessors, so fine an instrument should have been suffered to lie idle in a cabinet, as though it were a picture to be looked at, but not touched. From its condition, however, it is clear that it had always been in hands that prized it, for he describes it as having quite the appearance of a new instrument. In this respect, therefore, we must still adopt the opinion of the most eminent judges, including that recorded by Spohr, that it requires both time and use to perfect all instruments of the violin class. It would appear moreover that this has always been a settled belief, for even Mace in his "Music's Monument," published in 1676, says " We chiefly value old instruments before new for by experience they are found to be far the best." As to the condition of this instrument which Fetis states to be quite unique for its perfection and apparent newness, our countryman, Mr. Gardiner, in his interesting work, " Music and Friends," says that Mr. Champion, an amateur had given 300 guineas for a Stradiuarius violin and tenor, of a beautiful yellow colour inclining to orange, and which appeared to have been untouched since the day they were made. Here then in this country is a double instance of the same fact as to condition, for which M. Fetis claims for the Paris instrument the title of unique. The fact is that these fine violins have for many years been so highly appreciated that their possessors have taken the most extraordinary care to prevent their being damaged or disfigured, and there are many instances of violins in equally perfect condition.

After 1725, at which date Stradiuarius was 80 years old, his work lost some of its characteristic excellence though still of great merit. His sons, Homobono and Francesco, now assisted him, but he appears still to have signed them, occasionally adding to their names however, the words *sub disciplina A. Stradiuarius*. He had many pupils, the chief and the best of whom was Carlo Bergonzi. There were also Gobetti of Venice, Guadagnini of Cremona. Michael Angelo Bergonzi, and others mentioned in the dictionary. Fine examples of the works of his pupils are now becoming very valuable, and are well worthy attention.

Stradiuarius made a few instruments inlaid with ebony and ivory round the edges. There is a quartett of them, all bearing the same date 1687. One is in the collection of Charles Plowden, Esq.; the other violin belongs to a gentleman in Staffordshire; the violoncello belongs to the Queen of Spain, and the tenor was once the property of Sir Wm. Curtis. This is a very curious and remarkable set of instruments, very highly finished and in fine preservation. There is also another violin inlaid which belonged to the late Dr. Camidge of York, bearing date 1713. A. Fountain, Esq., has in his possession the last violin which Stradiuarius made. This instrument is known as the Habenock Violin from the previous owner's name from whom Mr. Fountain had it. Charles Plowden, Esq., has a quartett of splendid instruments by Stradiuarius, of which one violin is of the Grand Pattern, dated 1710; another dated 1711; which are perfect in model and preservation, and both first-class; the third is a remarkable violin, with rich golden varnish, dated 1709—a perfect instrument, which has been twice sold for £600, was formerly the property of Emiliani and is still known by his name. The fourth violin is the inlaid instrument mentioned above. Besides these, Mr. Plowden possesses a magnificent violoncello by Stradiuarius—a remarkable specimen both for beauty and tone; and also, four violins by Joseph Guarnerius which will be mentioned under the head of that master.

There is in Derbyshire a very fine Stradiuarius which was purchased by Viotti for his friend Mr. Hankey, from whom this and the Amati mentioned elsewhere went to his brother, a distinguished amateur, who died some years ago. Wm. Howard, Esq., of Sheffield, has a fine Stradiuarius violin, of the most beautiful yellow varnish, splendid wood, fine tone, and perfect condition, which formerly belonged to Salomon.

We may also mention here that the late eminent violinist Ernst, played upon a very fine Stradiuarius Violin which was presented to him by A. Fountain, Esq., an ardent admirer of that famous player. Joachim also uses a Stradiuarius. Servais, the great French performer, uses a Stradiuarius Violoncello, which is said to be the handsomest known, and which cost him 500 guineas.

The value of the best productions of the genius of Stradiuarius is now very great. Mr. Betts, of London, had one for which he refused the enormous sum of £500, and Dragonetti also refused £800 for a double bass. The highest price, £600 however was given twice for the violin now belonging to Mr. Plowden. But even such prices have been exceeded by that of the celebrated King Joseph Guarnerius mentioned elsewhere, which realised £700. It must not be understood however that such prices are the rule, for it is only for extraordinary specimens that any such great sum can be obtained. Excellent instruments are frequently sold for much smaller amounts, and it must also be remembered that none but those made from about 1700 to 1725 realise such enormous sums. His earlier productions, which resemble those of his master, and which are known by the name of Stradiuarius Amatis, can be had occasionally for moderate prices. An undoubted violin of any period of this great master's make, is well worthy the attention of the virtuoso. They are all good, but the grand pattern of this wonderful genius, possessing equal sweetness with greatly increased power, are only now to be had by connoisseurs of unlimited means.

As an illustration of the more moderate prices which these fine productions command, we think it may interest our readers to give here the result of a public sale of Cremona instruments belonging to the Count de Castelbarco of Milan, a distinguished amateur. M. Fetis in his work states that the Count possessed " two quartetts of Stradiuarius, very remarkable instruments; another of Joseph Guarnerius; a fourth of Nicholas Amati, and lastly a quartett of Steiner," of which he specially particularises the Tenor as " being a model of perfection as to workmanship, and the tone of which is of extreme beauty." These instruments were sold by auction by Messrs. Puttick and Simpson, on the 26th June, 1862. We quote the report of the " Times," by which it will be seen that our English connoisseurs did not appreciate them so highly as M. Fetis. The " Times" did not mention the Guarnerii and the Steiner at all, we presume because the prices were nothing remarkable.

LOT.
1	Violin by Stradiuarius,	1712	£70
2	Do.	do.	1699	£56
5	Tenor	do.	1715	£100
6	Violin	do.	1701	£135
8	Do.	do.	1685	£135
9	Do.	do.	1713	£90
12	Do.	Nicholas Amati,	....39 gs.
13	Do.	Andrew Amati	........36 gs.
26	Violoncello, Stradiuarius	1697	£210
28	Do.	do.	1687	£115
30	Do.—Nicholas Amati	1687	£130
31	Original Letter by Stradiuarius £8

At the same sale a Grand Amati Violin, jewelled at the corners, £60; Violin by Guarnerius, 38 guineas.

In addition to the above we may mention that the Stradiuarius Violin, which once belonged to a member of the Medici Family, was sold by auction a short time ago, at the Hotel de Drouet in Paris, for 5,745f., about £230, an excellent price for a Parisian connoisseur. We have already mentioned many fine instruments by Stradiuarius which are in the hands of connoisseurs and performers. We will now mention a fact which in the estimation of all true lovers of these fine violins is to be greatly regretted. It is not the only instance, as probably our readers are aware that the celebrated Guarnerius Violin of Paganini, is now locked up in a museum at Genoa. There is at a museum in the city of Florence, a quartett of beautiful instruments by Stradiuarius, consisting of two violins, tenor, and violoncello, which were presented to the institution by an Italian Nobleman, whose ancestors purchased them from the master himself. These instruments are most beautiful and in the highest preservation. But of all other curiosities, Cremona Violins are the most unsuitable for a museum, because they lie there dead, and are no more than names. The soul of music which is embodied in them is imprisoned within wood and crystal, and is no more heard of men. Let no one leave his Cremona to a museum.

Before closing our account of this great master, it may not be uninteresting to state that in his life time, he appears to have charged about £1 for a violin, and that he made so many during the course of his long and industrious career, that his fellow citizens spoke of him as rich. "As rich as Stradiuarius," was a common remark, as we see by M. Fetis' notice. Another anecdote is, that Cervetto, an Italian merchant in London, had a consignment of violins from the master himself, and as he could not get four pounds each for them he returned them. This appears strongly to disprove the assertion that his instruments were as good when made as they are now, especially when we find that in 1662, £40 was given for two Cremona violins for King Charles' band, no doubt the elder Amati's, which at that date would be getting mellowed by time. It is clear that King Charles, or the leader of his band, knew the value of Cremona instruments, for reckoning the difference in the value of money at the two periods, £20 then would purchase £120 worth of goods now. It is therefore extraordinary that if they were as good new as when they are old, the paltry sum of four pounds could not be got for them. The real truth no doubt is that whoever the maker, time must be the refiner, and even genius like that of Stradiuarius and Guarnerius could not impart that grand, rich, and mellow tone which distinguishes them without the aid of old Father Time.

The Cremona Varnish.

Those who desire to make themselves acquainted with the chief characteristics of the great Cremona makers should take every opportunity of examining genuine instruments. In addition to the other external indications we have pointed out, one of the most important, which is also the most difficult, if not impossible to imitate, is the varnish, including the colour. None of them seem to have adhered to one colour only. The present master for instance covered some of his finest violins with a deep rich yellow, almost approaching to orange. Others again will be found of a fine red, having something of a most lovely light cherry tint. Now these colours were mixed by the best makers with amber varnish of the purest and clearest consistency, and both colours and varnish are perfectly free from that muddy sort of appearance which so often disfigures modern instruments.

The effect is that of perfect transparency. You look at a clear perfect rich colour, as it were, through the purest crystal. This is one of the most certain indications of a genuine instrument. The moderns unfortunately seem to have lost the secret of making this lovely transparent clear coloured varnish, and the consequence is that a connoisseur of ability and experience never doubts when he sees an instrument whether it be the work of a great master. It is however supposed that all the genuine productions of the chief Cremona makers are now known, and we would not therefore have our readers flatter themselves they can pick up any of them in a casual way. Vigilant eyes and sharp judgments have long swept over Europe in search of them. But the advantage is this—that a knowledge of the best enables the amateur to discern a near approach to it, and thus distinguish those makers who are not so well known, though, being the pupils and followers of the great masters, they are well worthy of his choice. Large diamonds are rare and very dear. A smaller gem must suffice the amateur of moderate means.

THE GUARNERIUS FAMILY.

This is another glorious name in the annals of Cremona. Many of the first connoisseurs, now hesitate whether to apply the epithet greatest to Guarnerius or to Stradiuarius. The palm is therefore divided between them. Certain it is however that inasmuch as money rules the world, if we resort to that test, Guarnerius is the brightest gem, for it is recorded that he has sold for £700 and Stradiuarius for only £600. Most of the rich connoisseurs therefore desire to possess both. The great players, to whom money is more an object, divide their affections between them, and are satisfied with either one or the other, as chance or opportunity may decide.

The first of this celebrated family was Andreas, who was born in 1630 and died about

1695. He appears to have been a pupil of Nicholas Amati, and shows much of his teacher's careful finish. His instruments are generally beautifully made, of good and handsome wood, with excellent varnish, principally of amber colour like that of the Amatis. He also occasionally, but much more seldom, used red coloured varnish. This artiste is not famous for producing a great tone in his instruments, and he is therefore not elevated to the first class, but he made very good violins which are well worthy the attention of the amateur. We have seen a very fine specimen in the hands of A. Bright, Esq., of Sheffield, which was purchased of Mr. Hart, and which is decidedly the best instrument we have seen of this master. It is remarkably handsome, of a beautiful yellow colour, the back of one piece with rather small figure, the ribs similar, the head most carefully and accurately formed and the belly of fine wood. The tone is also more powerful than Andrew's violins generally are, and it is altogether a very fine example of his work.

GUISEPPE GUARNERIUS is considered to be the son of Andrew, and his instruments are generally signed as fiilius Andræ, very probably to distinguish him from his more celebrated cousin and namesake, who is besides generally known by the name of Joseph del Gesu. Guiseppe's instruments are very similar to his cousin's in quality—but less powerful and probably not so round in tone. They have however, a firm well defined kind of sound, which is always pleasing both to the player and the hearer, the former never feeling that the tone will give way under his bow. There are a great number with "slab" backs. The varnish is of first quality, and his violins are yearly becoming more valuable and of greater importance. We have seen a violoncello by this master, which is very fine. The back, ribs and head of very beautiful small figured wood. The belly of very fine grained wood, the bate looking like fine threads of silk stretched at regular intervals the whole width and length of the instrument, and with an exceedingly rich red varnish. It possesses also a fine quality of tone, and is dated 1713.

PIETRO, another son of Andreas, dates from 1690 to 1720. In the latter part of his life, he appears to have removed from Cremona to Mantua, his labels bearing date from thence. He was a pupil of his father, but is said not to have equalled him in careful finish. His instruments, however, command considerable respect and fetch a good price, a violoncello of his being recorded to have sold a few years ago for £120.

JOSEPH, nephew of Andreas, born in 1683, and died in 1745, is the last and best of the race of violin makers of this name. He was distinguished by the title of Joseph del Gesu, through his using on his labels, the monogram I.H.S., with a cross over or through the H. His career appears to have been of a very chequered complexion. From all the accounts that have come down to us, he seems to have been a man of irregular habits and eccentric genius. In consequence of these peculiarities, his instruments differ greatly in their characteristics. Neither the model, the wood, nor the varnish possesses much verisimilitude at different periods of his career. They are all, however, marked by the stamp of genius, and give but little trouble to a well informed connoisseur. Even under the most distressing circumstances, when on some account, he was confined in prison, and was obliged to be indebted to his goaler's daughter for the materials with which he worked, they still bear the characteristics and originality of a great master. The finish, however, of those which he made at this period was inferior to the others, being rather coarse and slovenly, and the work altogether little indicating externally the signs of that real excellence which they possess. At his best period, however, his instruments are of rare beauty and merit, and equal or perhaps excel those of Stradinarius. The wood he then used was of fine quality, and the varnish rich and lustrous and very often of similar lovely tints as those of that master. Many of his instruments are of rather small pattern, but in his best period, he produced some of large size and of extraordinary power and grandeur of tone. Among them was the famous favourite violin of Paganini, the renown of which, says M. Vuillaume, " was equal to that of its master."

This was the instrument on which, the most celebrated of all violin players the world ever saw, produced those extraordinary effects which astonished the whole musical world, and which will never be forgotten by those who heard them, nor perhaps excelled by any other. These instruments are however unfortunately very rare, and as rich connoisseurs will have them if possible, the value of them has come to be very great. We have elsewhere mentioned the magnificent violin known by the name of the King Joseph Guarnerius, for which Mr. Hart received the enormous sum of £700, which is the largest amount ever obtained for a violin on record. This splendid violin is of large pattern, with beautiful rich orange yellow varnish and splendid wood. It was imported into this country by Mr. Hart, and has been in the hands of those enthusiastic and judicious collectors, Mr. James Goding and Mr. Stewart. Joseph Guarnerius appears to have endeavoured to produce the grandest tone, combining majesty and refinement. Many people think he did so without thought or design, but we think otherwise. In the first place he seems to have fixed on Gaspar di Salo and Magini as his models, for if a comparison be made we shall find there are many points which resemble these instruments, for example, the peculiar shaped sound holes, the manner in which they are placed and the flat model, all of which tend to produce power, while he obtained the quality from the wonderful ingenuity he exercised in leaving the thicknesses of the wood in evidently the correct places, which was the necessary step in advance. He certainly made many rough instruments which are ascribed to his imprisonment, and which are now called the Prison Guarnerii, but the varnish on these even is not surpassed. He made many of a rich yellow colour, and others of red, the latter of which are matchless instruments. His heads are not finely cut, but the character he gave them has never been excelled.

In the first rank of Joseph Guarnerius instruments we must no doubt place that belonging to Paganini, which would, if it could be obtained, command an extraordinary price, and there are also many other noble productions of his skill extant. The King Joseph Guarnerius we have before mentioned. Mr. Plowden has four very valuable violins by this master. One was formerly the property of Mr. Goding, and was esteemed by him the finest in his collection. Another is quite equal, more highly finished and has his splendid red varnish. The third was formerly the property of Ole Bull, and is considered of the finest model of the master in his more unfinished and larger sized instruments, dated 1714. The fourth, less well known, but perhaps more perfect, certainly in tone, 1742. These four instruments are considered by most of the virtuosi, to be probably the finest examples extant of this great master. Certainly there are few collectors who can boast of having so many fine violins as these four by Guarnerius, and the four by Stradinarius previously described. Mr. Plowden has always gone on the principle of getting the very best instruments of each master, and his taste and judgment are well evidenced in his collection. The late Earl of Falmouth possessed some very valuable instruments such as the Kiesewetter Guarnerius and the Jarnovick Guarnerius, so named after their owners, and also a fine Magini Tenor, all of which were purchased by Mr. Hart.

The late lamented Prince Consort had a very fine tenor by Joseph Guarnerius, which was highly finished and had belonged to Dragonetti. There are many other fine specimens of Guarnerius in this country. English collectors, with that splendid contempt for cost which distinguishes them, allow no fine instruments to leave the country if they know it, and the consequence is that in the present day, and for some time back, England ranks first in the number and value of the Cremona Violins she possesses. Next comes France, who has some able connoisseurs; then Russia and Germany. Italy, strange to say, has suffered them all to leave her, and though the native country of Stradiuarius and Guarnerius, it is doubtful whether other nations have not attracted all the finest instruments out of her own possession. The great rise in the value of these extraordinary instruments is no doubt due to the fact that they were built very strong in wood, the effect of which would be to depreciate the tone when they were built, but which, now time has ameliorated them and the wood has become capable of free vibration, has refined the quality and increased the tone. Fifty years ago, a Guarnerius of the best time might have been bought for £50 that will now command £500. Neither does it appear that they have yet reached their climax, for they are yearly increasing in value as the examples we have mentioned clearly show.

THE GREAT TYROLESE MAKER.
JACOB STEINER.

The time has been when the instruments of this master, whose name is perhaps yet as widely known as the Cremonese, were very highly esteemed in England. In Germany it is so yet, and many of the amateurs of that country flatter themselves that Steiner ranks first in the roll of famous violin makers. Their celebrated violinist, Spohr, however, in his remarks on the subject inserted in his Violin School does not coincide with the opinion of his fellow countrymen to this effect, for he puts Steiner in the second rank, reserving to the first Nicholas Amati, Antonius Stradiuarius, and Joseph Guarnerius. In this decision he also generally expresses the opinion of the travelled professional violinists of his own country as well as all Europe. But it is well known that in Germany a well preserved instrument of Steiner's best period will sell for much more money than any where else. In England more especially we adopt exactly the reverse valuation. Steiner will not now command a greater price than many of the pupils of the great masters, and perhaps to some extent this may arise from the immense number of spurious instruments bearing his name, which the inferior Tyrolese makers put forth to the world and palmed on a credulous public as his genuine instruments. Perhaps no master has been more copied and imitated, both in Germany and elsewhere. In England the violin makers in the beginning of the eighteenth century, mostly copied the pattern and model of Steiner. There must, therefore, be some good and powerful reason for this general depreciation in value and reputation which Steiner has suffered. This the candid inquirer readily finds in the fact that the instruments of Steiner, which were generally constructed on a high and peculiar model were only calculated for the production of a thin though sparkling tone, while the Italians aimed, particularly in the flatter instruments, to obtain a full rich and round tone. This distinction is apparent even in the older Cremona makers, but if we compare those of Steiner with those of Nicholas Amati, of Stradiuarius, or Guarnerius, the thin tone of the former and the rich round tone of the latter become instantly most striking. The consequence is that the rich amateurs who form collections, and the great performers whose interest it is to please by the quality of tone as well as the grace and finish of their execution, no longer purchase the Steiner violins except as matters of curiosity in the case of a very fine example. We do not know any great player who uses a Steiner instrument, as we shall show in another article. We therefore only now class Steiner among the great masters, from his past reputation, and for certain special instruments.

Jacob Steiner was a native of the Tyrol, and was born at Absom, near Inspruck, about 1620. It is said that an old instrument by

s

Kerlino, which he found in the house, gave him his first tendencies towards the art of violin making. Certain it is however that while yet a youth he obtained employment in the workshop of Nicholas Amati. This was an excellent school for the young aspirant, and after some years he made some instruments which, with the exception of sixteen which will be mentioned later, are considered to be the finest specimens of his talent. These fine violins are the product of his Cremonese inspiration, and bear a written label signed by himself and dated from Cremona about 1644. These instruments are modelled higher than those of his master, thus showing a singular divergence from the principle of gradual decrease in the height of the model of the Amatis, from Andrew to Nicholas. This divergence from that principle, which ended in the flat model of Stradinarius, must be considered to be the real cause of the loss of favour which the Steiner violins, though beautiful in other respects, have undergone. Steiner exaggerated the old practice instead of following the new lights of science, and while

the latter have yielded the brightest results,
the former has tarnished the real talent of this
otherwise excellent artiste. Probably another
reason for the defective tone of Steiner's instruments in comparison with the Cremonese and Brescian, is the practice of model-
ling his violins with an extraordinary and peculiar rise to about the foot of the bridge, and
then keeping it nearly flat. Otto describes it
thus, "the breadth of this raised part is about
the same as the bridge itself, and then it falls
off towards the edges. The model is precisely
similar towards the neck and on the broad
part (beneath the finger board.") This description is only imperfect in this point that
sufficient stress is not laid on the words *fall
off*. It is literally a falling off, and on the
principles of acoustics must of necessity make
the tone thin. Andrew Amati, on the contrary, built nearly as high, but beautifully and
gradually sloped them down to the purfling,
and his instruments, though small in tone, are
yet full, round and sweet. In other respects
Steiner at this period was a most careful
maker, and his instruments show very fine

finish and workmanship. They are of the small pattern, with the S holes rather shorter than the Cremonas, somewhat narrow and beautifully formed ; the head also smaller and particularly round and smooth. The varnish is similar to that of the Amatis, and the wood of the belly has a fine open grain.

After the production of these instruments at Cremona, Steiner removed to his native place and having married the daughter of Antonius Amati appears to have lost his ambition, and made many very inferior instruments. His history at this period is somewhat melancholy. Pressed by the necessities of a family and the want of active patronage, his genius languished and he became negligent and careless in his work. This continued for some time till fortune again smiled upon him, when not being compelled to sell for immediate wants he again resumed his careful finish and began to be distinguished as a good maker. At about this period Klotz and Albani became his pupils, and he produced some excellent instruments, which are often distinguished by the scrolls being ornamented with lions heads which are beautifully carved. These and the heads of other animals are supposed to denote the crests of his patrons at this period. They are dated from about 1650 to 1667 at Absom. Fetis says the French violinist, Alard, has a violin of this period of the greatest beauty, and that there is in Paris a genuine Steiner, which he has heard Sivori play upon, which although of a very small pattern has an unusually brilliant tone.

Now comes the most brilliant period of this artiste's history in a musical sense, though somewhat romantic and mysterious otherwise.

Retiring to a monastery, it is said after the death of his wife, he there passed the remainder of his life, but there does not appear to be any positive information when he died. While there, however, he resolved to distinguish the close of his career by the construction of some violins of super-eminent beauty and quality. This he accomplished by the aid of the superior, who obtained for him some very fine wood, out of which those most famous instruments, known by the name of *Elector Steiners* were made by him. These are the violins which by common consent most entitle this artiste to rank with the great masters. They are of the very highest quality of the Steiner tone, which Dubourg describes as "a pure ringing ethereal tone, comparable to that of a woman's perfect voice—a shape of elegance—studied finish in every detail, and a diaphonous varnish of golden hue." Such are the characteristics, says this enthusiastic admirer of these productions of Steiner's third or last epoch. There were sixteen of these violins, one of which he presented to each of the twelve Electors, and the remaining four to the Emperor. Unfortunately thirteen of them appear to have been lost, and the remainder have all been in royal hands, the Empress Maria Theresa, the Duke of Orleans, grandfather of King Louis Philippe, and Frederick William of Prussia, and been presented by them (except the last) to eminent foreign violinists.

We have now presented a concise sketch of the career of this celebrated artiste, and it is to be regretted that none of his more celebrated violins are known to be in this country, to enable us to judge more accurately, whether he succeeded, in any of them, in producing any close approximation to the rich round tone of the best Cremona makers. The best of those known to English connoisseurs are characterised by the thin though brilliant tone we have described, which, when compared with the Italian masterpieces, has led to their general depreciation in the estimation of the highest authorities and the most distinguished performers on the violin.

WHY ARE CERTAIN VIOLINS OF MORE VALUE THAN OTHERS?

In considering this question, several difficulties present themselves to the inquirer. We are all aware of the infinite diversity of tastes in the first instance, and in the next, accurate judgment is a matter which depends on the union of so many qualities that it is rare indeed to find two opinions completely alike. Nevertheless we do find that there are a few instruments which by universal consent have become the standard of taste. They are " the glass of fashion and the mould of form" in the violin world. An appeal to these famous violins must therefore be of some service in this inquiry, which is of very considerable importance, because its object is to decide what is that tone which confers that immense value which some violins have realised as distinguished from that which possesses only a merit of so inferior a character as to become scarcely valuable in any degree. In other words, what are the distinguishing characteristics of tone of the violins made by Nicholas Amati, Antonius Stradiuarius, and Joseph Guarnerius. These three makers are now the Raphaels, the Titians, and the Claudes of the musical world, and a few thoughts on their works in connection with this subject may help us to a decision on this difficult point, at least to the great bulk of amateurs. We will divide the inquiry into three heads.

1. Power.
2. Sweetness.
3. Purity.

In considering the first point, power, the amateur will have to beware of a very possible mistake he may fall into. There is *apparent* power under the ear, arising from coarseness. This is a species of power which is observable chiefly by the player. The listener, especially if at a little distance, does not hear this power. The tone is clogged and thickened with the resinous particles which have remained in the wood and which perhaps, from its nature may never leave it altogether, and the vibration is not therefore perfect. Another cause of false power is a certain imperfect build wherein the parts are not properly calculated as in the fine Cremona productions. These two classes of instruments are very apt to deceive unpractised ears. But a moment's comparison with one of the genuine great masters will show them in a most unmistakable manner the difference. What then is real power? It is simply musical tone, divested of all adventitious qualities. When tone of this class is heard near, the effect is charming to the ear. When heard afar off, it seems to swell out and become magnificent and telling. Who that has heard a great player on a fine instrument, that has not been astonished at the immense quantity of tone which arises from this exceedingly fine quality. And it is in this way that even the small Amatis, built when great amount of tone was not wanted and would not have been appreciated, are still most delightful as solo instruments. Its purity and fine quality carry it to a much greater distance and produce a greater effect, than would arise from larger instruments of less careful build and euphonic qualities. Herein is discovered the difference between violins of the three great masters named and others of the same name. If a small Nicholas Amati be compared with a large model, it will be found that the quality is similar, but the quantity is greater, and therefore the instrument becomes more valuable. Again, in a Stradiuarius or Joseph Guarnerius of the best period, which are of the flat model and most accurate build, we find a pure ringing and deliciously rich quality, without roughness or coarseness, that finds its way through everything to a great distance, even in a crowded concert room. The differences in the three great makers seems to be now decided to consist in fullness of tone and quantity of power. The Amatis are essentially sweet and vocal. The Stradiuarius—of similar quality, greatly increased in body and of a more ringing bell-like character. The Guarnerius of the best model is even still more powerful. But they all possess that essential purity and richness of tone without which there is no real excellence. On this head we find, therefore, that power, providing it be accompanied by the other essentials of sweetness and purity, confers on violins the greatest value. A Nicholas Amati of the grand pattern—a Stradiuarius of the large flat model, or a Guarnerius of similar characteristics—all of which have been built with the greatest care and attention to the resonant qualities of the wood, and possess all these essentials—are therefore the instruments that have and will always command the greatest admiration.

The next essential point in a good instrument we have to consider is sweetness. This combines characteristics which are not essential to power. A violin may possess the latter without the former. The tone may be of a quality which will tell and carry, but not of that soft delicious voice like nature which we call sweetness. The most admirable instruments of this characteristic have been variously compared to a flute or to the female voice. The latter is the best comparison. For the brightest examples of this quality alone we must look to the small violins of Antonius and Hieronymus, and also of Nicholas Amati. They are of the most delicious quality, and for solo instruments cannot be excelled. They respond with the most charming effect to the most touching and passionate expression. A great player can really sing on these with such a delightful effect as almost to compensate for the want of speech.

The third point is purity of tone. We may be said to have touched upon this already in treating of the other two. But it is necessary to allude to this also, because it is possible to have purity of tone without sweetness or power. There are many instruments which from age and use have lost all harshness or roughness of tone, but are still of a thin piercing quality. These may be said to be pure in tone, but not possessing the other requisites they fail in commanding attention. What we have to look for in a violin is that roundness and fullness of quality which are combined in the term sweetness. Tone cannot be said to be sweet which is thin or piercing. It lacks one essential characteristic. It is on this account that in the present day many of the Steiner instruments have lost favour. There are a few which possess both sweetness and purity, and they rank with the small Amatis. But the best of them are wanting in power. This characteristic is only heard in perfection in the Stradiuarius or the Guarnerius of Cremona, and the great Brescian makers Gaspar di Salo and Magini. An amateur should look therefore in purchasing an instrument whether it possesses these three characteristics or any or which of them.

We have now shown what are the essentials of a fine instrument, but as the genuine productions of these great masters are mostly in the hands of rich amateurs it is scarcely possible to become the happy possessor of one of the perfect instruments. What then shall we do? The reply is simple. Study the characteristics we have described, and you will find in some of the pupils of the Amati, Stradiuarius, or Guarnerius a near approach to this excellence. In fact it is well known that in the scarcity of originals fine examples by the pupils have frequently been sold as the work of the masters themselves. The Dictionary we have compiled will tell the amateur what names will most probably supply the qualities he desires. Care and attention will do the rest.

ON THE PRODUCTION

OF

GOOD TONE IN VIOLINS.

In the preceding chapter we have endeavoured to solve the question what are the qualities that constitute good tone. We now propose to inquire how good tone is provided for in the construction of the violin. We are not about to enter into the scientific question. We wish merely to give to the general amateur a knowledge which is often only acquired after years of patient study and trial of instruments, by certain general principles which will seldom or never be found to be incorrect in fact, and then only through instruments being built on false rules in other respects. In good instruments these rules may be said to be infallible.

It is a curious fact that Gaspar di Salo and Magini, both early makers, started with the principle which has since been brought to the greatest perfection by the Cremona makers, and built on the flat model. Their instruments are consequently found to possess much of the fine and powerful tone which distinguishes Stradiuarius and Guarnerius. The early Amatis, in the second place, built on a higher model, and their instruments possess a sweet but not powerful tone. Steiner, thirdly, built on a higher model still, and his instruments have a thin piercing tone. We can only draw one conclusion from these facts—namely, that the nearer we approach an entire flat in the model of a violin the fuller, rounder, and more powerful the tone; other points of careful work and good varnish being taken into consideration. This fact has strongly impressed itself on the minds of scientific inquirers, and the result has been, as tests of the principle, the production of flat violins. These have been tried and reported satisfactory in the matter of tone. But there are other points to provide for which a flat box does not allow. To gain the requisite mass of air to produce good tone a flat violin has to be made of a clumsy awkward shape. In the beautiful modelled violin this is provided for in the rise of the back and belly. The ribs may therefore be more or less shallow according to the height of the model, and yet provide a sufficient space for the necessary amount of air for the production of good tone. We arrive then at this one certain fact, that the flatter the model of a violin the greater the probability of a good fine tone. It is of such violins therefore that we find the great performers possess themselves. This may be said to be an infallible rule, and an examination of the instruments of the most celebrated makers fully confirms it.

Why therefore did the elder Amati, contemporary and probably pupil of Gaspar di Salo, change the model and size of the instrument? This inquiry brings us to the second rule for the amateur. There cannot be a doubt that he adopted this plan because the flat model produced a more powerful tone than was then required. He therefore, no doubt acquainted practically, if not theoretically, with the principles of acoustics, raised his model and decreased his size to provide for the production of that eminently sweet tone which characterises his instruments. The amateur therefore who desires tone of this description, but does not want power, will generally find it in the model of medium height, providing as in all other cases, the work and the wood are good. Of this model are some of the sweetest toned violins to be found, of which the Amatis are the type.

Finally, many instruments are to be found constructed on Steiner's plan with very elevated model flat on the centre, and falling off abruptly towards the sides. These are all contrary to acoustic principles, and their thin piercing tone is to be ascribed to the want of that harmonious communication of vibration which their peculiar construction inevitably indicates.

Let, therefore, the amateur who wishes to be his own purveyor, examine, with these principles impressed on his mind, whatever instruments he can gain access to and the result will be that he will seldom err in this matter.

After this he must study the characteristics of good wood, careful finish, and fine varnish.

A knowledge of these is best acquired by examining the instruments of the great masters. To go fully into these also is not necessary here, having already commented on them under their respective heads. One remark is, however, necessary here. Many people foolishly imagine that *any* violin may be made to produce as sweet sounds in the hands of a skilful player as a high class instrument. This is a great mistake, and a convincing proof of its fallacy may be drawn from the fact that all the great soloists play upon high class violins. They do this moreover at a time when they would gladly save the expense were it possible. A few instances may interest the reader.

Great Players and their Instruments.

Joachim plays upon a Stradiuarius, Vieuxtemps on a Guarnerius, Ole Bull on a Guarnerius and an Amati, De Beriot on a Magini, (of which he had two very splendid examples, the second being now in the possession of the author,) Carrodus a Guarnerius, and many other living instances. Piatti a Ruggerius violoncello, Servais a Stradiuarius violoncello. Past examples may be cited in Paganini, who played upon a Guarnerius, Mori a Guarnerius, and Spagnoletti the same. Ernst used a Stradiuarius. Dragonetti played on a Gaspar di Salo and a Stradiuarius double bass.

GENERAL NOTES.

In the last article, we have given some general rules for judging of the probable tone of an instrument from its model. A few further remarks on this and other important topics will well supplement what we have said.

1.—Accurate judgment in violins can only be obtained by long experience and seeing many instruments, and if possible those of a high class. There are many little points which to a casual or careless observer are invisible, but which a practised connoisseur detects immediately, and thereby is enabled to declare the maker. A difficulty will often present itself to a tyro in the knowledge of violins, from the family likeness which it is possible to trace, for example, between Amati, Stradiuarius and Bergonzi. These have a general resemblance which indicates the coming from one school. This applies also in many other cases—but every master has some distinct difference which is perceptible to the practised eye. The faces of a flock of sheep are to a stranger all alike; to the shepherd, each has its personal individuality. It is the same with violins, which can be read by the practised student as easily as we know each other by the countenance.

2.—It is erroneous to imagine that Cremonese instruments can be successfully imitated, a very popular story about Paganini's Guarnerius to the contrary notwithstanding, as the lawyers say. An attempt to impose an imitation on a practised judge is always productive of an unpleasant result. To fall from the sublime to the ridiculous is especially awkward, and results in becoming very particularly ridiculous yourself. This *must* be whenever a modern maker attempts to make an ancient violin. There are practical difficulties impossible now to get over—such as the varnish. The secret of making the grand old varnish is lost, and therefore whatever is put on by a modern tells the tale and cries aloud to the judge—This is a cheat!

3.—It is easier to imitate an old painting than an old violin, though that is difficult enough to a good judge, but such an insuperable obstacle as the old amber varnish does not puzzle the picture forger.

4.—In choosing an instrument it is better to select one of a flat model, the sides of medium height, well proportioned and with good oil varnish.

5.—We are inclined to think that all the great instruments of the great makers are well known, and that there are none lying by unknown to fame.

6.—Most of the more celebrated instruments are given a name of distinction, such as the Yellow Stradiuarius, the Blood Red Knight Guarnerius, the Ole Bull Guarnerius. the De Beriot Magini, the Emmeliani Stradiuarius, the General Kidd Stradiuarius Violoncello, the Servais Stradiuarius Violoncello, and others. These can be recognised like the human face.

7.—The reason why Italian instruments are so superior to all others must be ascribed to their exquisite make, the careful adjustment of the various thicknesses of wood and the varnish, the secret of which appears gone for ever. Perhaps another reason may be named in the wood being so ripe and dry as to permit free vibration.

8.—The Cremonese obtained their colour in oil. The moderns get it only in spirit, which imparts a hardness to the tone. Compare a Cremona with the German and other imitations. Can't you hear how perceptible the difference? The former is mellow and rich—the latter flinty and harsh. This arises no doubt from the varnish.

9.—The Cremonese violoncellos were mostly made deeper by half an inch at the bottom than at the upper part. Guiseppe fil Andreæ, Guarnerius, Stradiuarius, Landulphus, and others observed this rule. The tone is said to be greatly improved by it.

10.—Some persons think it is very difficult to obtain an Italian violin at a moderate price. It is not so. There are many whose makers are not known, and also third class instruments of good qualities, which can be obtained from

£10 to £25. It is better to purchase one of these than a baked copy or a new violin. Then again amateurs may resort to the old French makers, some old English and the Tyrolean, which may be had cheaper still.

11.—A respectable dealer who is known to be a connoisseur of experience, will never sell you a modern copy for an old Italian violin with a long story of how he got it in some wonderful way. His character is at stake. Beware of ignorance which assumes the mask of knowledge, or of designing roguery which apes the appearance of innocence.

12.—The present excellence of the old instruments arises from their having been made thick in wood, which time has ameliorated and mellowed, and now permits free vibration. It is much to be deplored that many instruments have not been suffered to remain as the makers left them, and that others under a false notion of giving an old tone have been made too thin.

13.—Had Magini, Gaspar di Salo, and other very old makers used as little wood as some of their successors, where would their instruments have been now? We are at the present time reaping the benefit of their foresight.

14.—There is evident proof of the deep interest the high class makers took in endeavouring to advance the interests of their art. For example, Stradiuarius sometimes put the widest grained wood on the fourth string side, feeling it was the weakest and needed the open grain. Sometimes he put it on the first string side. He was evidently trying experiments. But he mostly adopted the former plan, no doubt correctly. Again, they made instruments larger at the bottom than at the upper part, gradually reducing in size and depth, an experiment which observation has since found to be correct. They also made instruments thicker under the bridge to enable them to bear the great tension to which they are subject, and many other points showing how perfect they became. They left little for modern ingenuity to discover.

15.—Old instruments of character should be greatly prized and carefully preserved, for it seems probable that there will be no others to take their places, from many well known causes.

16.—Makers of the present time have perverted their talents to discover a means of producing the qualities of old instruments in new ones, an achievement utterly impossible, as their efforts show. Many make instruments with the greatest care, copying the plans of the old masters—but instead of allowing Father Time to ripen them, they use an acid to dry up the wood, or bake them. These are known by a peculiar smell which tells the tale, and they get worse instead of better. Again, they deem it wise to get a colour at any price, which can only be done in our day by the use of spirit varnish. Did they use oil varnish, our successors would at all events reap the benefit, if not ourselves. The great masters were willing to wait for fame and tried none of these dodges. Others again put the varnish on and rub it off in places to resemble the wear of age. Much better would it be to cover the instrument with varnish and leave age to do the rest. Such schemes are futile and reflect discredit on those who adopt them.

17.—The peg holes seen in old Italian violoncellos in the middle of the back are where a peg was put to fasten the instrument round the neck while playing in the Catholic Churches.

18.—Stradiuarius in his early career frequently cut his wood to form what are called slab backs, (explained elsewhere,) and sometimes used pear tree for violoncellos.

REPAIRS OF INSTRUMENTS.

We cannot part with the reader who has thus far accompanied us in our labours, without making a few remarks on the important subject of repairs. So many fine instruments have been ruined and the beauty of so many more tarnished by the mal-addresse and ignorance of some so-called restorers and repairers, that we think we shall be serving the admirers of the violin by warning them against entrusting valuable instruments to incompetent hands. A few notes will serve to illustrate the chief subjects for care and some important items in fitting instruments properly.

1.—So-called repairs have been frequently so clumsily done, as to damage old and valuable instruments to an extent impossible to remedy.

REPAIRS OF INSTRUMENTS. 163

2.—There are many instances where wood has been taken out of the instrument under the idea of improving the tone. This is a fatal error, and when the mischief is discovered it is replaced by new wood. Others have done the same under another erroneous impression, that it will give strength to the instrument to enable it to bear the increased pressure caused by the higher pitch used at the present time. Whatever the notion, the result is always bad. The grain of the new wood does not come level with the old, and causes a sudden check to the vibration. The glue also lying between the old and the new wood deadens the sound. Some repairers have been guilty of this practice to a great extent, and many fine instruments have been thus damaged. Let no one under any plea tamper with the thicknesses of wood in a good violin.

3.—The sound bar used by the old masters (as we have before stated) and others of that period, was much shorter than is now used, and consequently all have been changed. The present bar is quite sufficient to bear the increased pressure required in our time, without resorting to any other means. If an alteration be required an experienced repairer only can know the kind of bar required.

4.—The necks of the old instruments were short; they have therefore to be lengthened if found in their old state. A good repairer will splice a neck in so as to be scarcely perceptible. Much of the ease and comfort of playing depends how this is done.

5.—The sound post is a very important item in fitting an instrument. There is a marvellous power in this simple contrivance. It should fit as though it were part of the back and belly. An instrument can be frequently cured of a bad description of tone by the slightest move of the post. Those subject to what are termed wolfy notes can be remedied or the bad notes shifted to less important ones. It is a mistake to suppose there is a particular place for the sound post in all instruments alike. It depends upon the model of the instrument to a great extent. High models require the post nearer the foot of the bridge than flat models. Others require the post thick or thin. The regulating of the post should only be entrusted to the skilled hand, and we would impress upon amateurs that it is better never to shift the post themselves. Many instruments have had the sound holes spoiled and the surface of the wood inside gored by unskilful tampering with the post.

6.—The bridge is another very important agent in regulating an instrument. No general rule will serve for this matter. Some instruments require the bridge thick, others thin. Some a close grain and others the contrary. The bridge should be fitted as accurately as the post, and as though it grew from the belly, the feet touching equally all round.

7.—Tail pieces are better quite free from ornaments, which frequently cause the instrument to jar disagreeably.

8.—The strings are of great importance. They should be adjusted to be in perfect fifths. This is essential, otherwise it is impossible to play double notes correctly in tune. It may be done with a little trouble. When the instrument is in tune on the open notes, place the finger across the strings, for example, at B on the second string, and F on the first string.

If the fifth is imperfect, tune one string a shade higher, and try again. If then perfect it requires a smaller string. If not, tune a shade lower than the perfect open fifth, if then right when tried as before, it requires a thicker string.*

---

* We have seen a little instrument advertised to accomplish this important matter without trouble.

THE PERFECT FIFTH'S GUAGE.—"This useful gauge is marked with such precision as to render all strings gauged by it in accordance with each other producing perfect fifths, enabling the performer to execute passages of double notes with the greatest facility and correctness, at the same time effecting a considerable saving of time and expense by entirely superseding the old method of obtaining fifths by changing the strings." It is manufactured and sold by Mr. John Hart, 14, Prince's-street, Leicester-square, London.

ADDENDA.

LARCHE, —— Brussels, 1847. Copyist of old makers. One of those who endeavoured to produce an old tone by the use of acid, and consequently spoiled the wood.

ALBANESI, —— Cremona, 1737. Similar to Testore of Milan, but broad pattern His instruments have a large tone, but poor varnish.

GOBIT, —— Venice, 1716. Made similar instruments to Ruggerius, and used beautiful varnish.

GABRIELLI, —— Florence, 1740. Made excellent Violoncellos, yellow varnish. Written labels.

ANTONIAZZI, GAETANO, Cremona, 1860. This maker sent a violin to the Exhibition of 1862, but is much behind his predecessors.

FALCO, —— Cremona, 1752. Made well proportioned instruments.

HARRIS, CHARLES, London. An admirable workman. His instruments are among the finest of the English.

GAGLIANO, NICHOLAS, Naples, pupil of Stradiuarius. We have a note (omitted in its proper place) that this maker excelled in violoncellos, many of which are covered with fine rich varnish, seldom seen on instruments by the Gagliano family.

In our notice of Stradiuarius Violins at page 113 we should have said that William Howard, Esq , of Sheffield, possessed *two* fine examples—one as described and the other of the beautiful red varnish, the latter formerly the property of the celebrated violinist Salomon, for whom Haydn wrote his twelve grand symphonies.

[JULY 1864.]

GENERAL LIST OF WORKS

PUBLISHED BY

MESSRS. LONGMAN, GREEN, AND CO.

PATERNOSTER ROW, LONDON.

Historical Works.

The **HISTORY of ENGLAND** from the Fall of Wolsey to the Death of Elizabeth. By JAMES ANTHONY FROUDE, M.A. late Fellow of Exeter College, Oxford. Third Edition of the First Eight Volumes.

    VOLS. I to IV. the Reign of Henry VIII. Third Edition, 54s.

    VOLS. V. and VI. the Reigns of Edward VI. and Mary. Third Edition, 28s.

    VOLS. VII. and VIII. the Reign of Elizabeth, VOLS. I. and II. Third Edition, 28s.

The **HISTORY of ENGLAND** from the Accession of James II. By Lord MACAULAY. Three Editions as follows.

    LIBRARY EDITION, 5 vols. 8vo. £4.

    CABINET EDITION, 8 vols. post 8vo. 48s.

    PEOPLE'S EDITION, 4 vols. crown 8vo. 16s.

REVOLUTIONS in ENGLISH HISTORY. By ROBERT VAUGHAN, D.D. 3 vols. 8vo. 45s.

    VOL. I. Revolutions of Race, 15s.

    VOL. II. Revolutions in Religion, 15s.

    VOL. III. Revolutions in Government, 15s.

The **HISTORY of ENGLAND** during the Reign of George the Third. By WILLIAM MASSEY, M.P. 4 vols. 8vo. 48s.

The **CONSTITUTIONAL HISTORY of ENGLAND**, since the Accession of George III. 1760—1860. By THOMAS ERSKINE MAY, C.B. 2 vols. 8vo. 33s.

LIVES of the QUEENS of ENGLAND, from State Papers and other Documentary Sources: comprising a Domestic History of England from the Conquest to the Death of Queen Anne. By AGNES STRICKLAND. Revised Edition, with many Portraits. 8 vols. post 8vo. 60s.

A

LECTURES on the HISTORY of ENGLAND. By WILLIAM LONG-
MAN. Vol. I. from the earliest times to the Death of King Edward II. with
6 Maps, a coloured Plate, and 53 Woodcuts. 8vo. 15s.

A CHRONICLE of ENGLAND, from B.C. 55 to A.D. 1485; written
and illustrated by J. E. DOYLE. With 81 Designs engraved on Wood and
printed in Colours by E. Evans. 4to. 42s.

HISTORY of CIVILISATION. By HENRY THOMAS BUCKLE. 2 vols.
Price £1 17s.

    VOL. I. *England and France,* Fourth Edition, 21s.

    VOL. II. *Spain and Scotland,* Second Edition, 16s.

DEMOCRACY in AMERICA. By ALEXIS DE TOCQUEVILLE. Translated by HENRY REEVE, with an Introductory Notice by the Translator.
2 vols. 8vo. 21s.

The SPANISH CONQUEST in AMERICA, and its Relation to the
History of Slavery and to the Government of Colonies. By ARTHUR HELPS.
4 vols. 8vo. £3. VOLS. I. and II. 28s. VOLS. III. and IV. 16s. each.

HISTORY of the REFORMATION in EUROPE in the Time of
Calvin. By J. H. MERLE D'AUBIGNE, D.D. VOLS. I. and II. 8vo. 28s. and
VOL. III. 12s.

LIBRARY HISTORY of FRANCE, in 5 vols. 8vo. By EYRE EVANS
CROWE. VOL. I. 14s. VOL. II. 15s. VOL. III. 18s. VOL. IV. nearly ready.

LECTURES on the HISTORY of FRANCE. By the late Sir JAMES
STEPHEN, LL.D. 2 vols. 8vo. 24s.

The HISTORY of GREECE. By C. THIRLWALL, D.D., Lord Bishop
of St. David's. 8 vols. 8vo. £3; or in 8 vols. fcp. 28s.

The TALE of the GREAT PERSIAN WAR, from the Histories of
Herodotus. By the Rev. G. W. Cox, M.A. late Scholar of Trin. Coll. Oxon.
Fcp. 8vo. 7s. 6d.

ANCIENT HISTORY of EGYPT, ASSYRIA, and BABYLONIA. By
the Author of 'Amy Herbert.' Fcp. 8vo. 6s.

CRITICAL HISTORY of the LANGUAGE and LITERATURE of
Ancient Greece. By WILLIAM MURE, of Caldwell. 5 vols. 8vo. £3 9s.

HISTORY of the LITERATURE of ANCIENT GREECE. By Professor K. O. MÜLLER. Translated by the Right Hon. Sir GEORGE CORNE-
WALL LEWIS, Bart. and by J.W. DONALDSON, D.D. 3 vols. 8vo. 36s.

HISTORY of the ROMANS under the EMPIRE. By the Rev
CHARLES MERIVALE, B.D. 7 vols. 8vo. with Maps, £5.

The FALL of the ROMAN REPUBLIC: a Short History of the Las
Century of the Commonwealth. By the Rev. CHARLES MERIVALE, B.I
12mo. 7s. 6d.

The BIOGRAPHICAL HISTORY of PHILOSOPHY, from its Origi.
in Greece to the Present Day. By GEORGE HENRY LEWES. Revised an
enlarged Edition. 8vo. 16s.

HISTORY of the INDUCTIVE SCIENCES. By WILLIAM WHEWEL]
D.D. F.R.S. Master of Trin. Coll. Cantab. Third Edition. 3 vols. crow
8vo. 24s.

CRITICAL and HISTORICAL ESSAYS contributed to the *Edinburgh Review*. By the Right Hon. LORD MACAULAY.
   LIBRARY EDITION, 3 vols. 8vo. 36s.
   TRAVELLER'S EDITION, in 1 vol. 21s.
   In POCKET VOLUMES, 3 vols. fcp. 21s.
   PEOPLE'S EDITION, 2 vols. crown 8vo. 8s.

EGYPT'S PLACE in UNIVERSAL HISTORY; an Historical Investigation. By C. C. J. BUNSEN, D.D. Translated by C. H. COTTRELL, M.A. With many Illustrations. 4 vols. 8vo. £5 8s. VOL. V. is nearly ready.

MAUNDER'S HISTORICAL TREASURY; comprising a General Introductory Outline of Universal History, and a series of Separate Histories. Fcp. 8vo. 10s.

HISTORICAL and CHRONOLOGICAL ENCYCLOPÆDIA, presenting in a brief and convenient form Chronological Notices of all the Great Events of Universal History. By B. B. WOODWARD, F.S.A. Librarian to the Queen.
                                            [*In the press.*

HISTORY of CHRISTIAN MISSIONS; their Agents and their Results By T. W. M. MARSHALL. 2 vols. 8vo. 24s.

HISTORY of the EARLY CHURCH, from the First Preaching of the Gospel to the Council of Nicæa, A.D. 325. By the Author of 'Amy Herbert.' Fcp. 8vo. 4s. 6d.

HISTORY of WESLEYAN METHODISM. By GEORGE SMITH, F.A.S. New Edition, with Portraits, in 31 parts. Price 6d. each.

HISTORY of MODERN MUSIC; a Course of Lectures delivered at the Royal Institution. By JOHN HULLAH, Professor of Vocal Music in King's College and in Queen's College, London. Post 8vo. 6s. 6d.

HISTORY of MEDICINE, from the Earliest Ages to the Present Time. By EDWARD MERYON, M.D. F.G.S. Vol. I. 8vo. 12s. 6d.

Biography and Memoirs.

SIR JOHN ELIOT, a Biography: 1590—1632. By JOHN FORSTER. With Two Portraits on Steel from the Originals at Port Eliot. 2 vols. crown 8vo. 30s.

LETTERS and LIFE of FRANCIS BACON, including all his Occasional Works. Collected and edited, with a Commentary, by J. SPEDDING, Trin. Coll. Cantab. VOLS. I. and II. 8vo. 24s.

LIFE of ROBERT STEPHENSON, F.R.S. By J. C. JEAFFRESON, Barrister-at-Law; and WILLIAM POLE, F.R.S. Memb. Inst. Civ. Eng. With 2 Portraits and many Illustrations. 2 vols. 8vo. [*Nearly ready.*

APOLOGIA pro VITA SUA: being a Reply to a Pamphlet entitled 'What then does Dr. Newman mean?' By JOHN HENRY NEWMAN, D.D. 8vo. 14s.

LIFE of the DUKE of WELLINGTON. By the Rev. G. R. GLEIG,
M.A. Popular Edition, carefully revised; with copious Additions. Crown
8vo. 5s.

Brialmont and Gleig's Life of the Duke of Wellington. 4 vols.
8vo. with Illustrations, £2 14s.

Life of the Duke of Wellington, partly from the French of M.
BRIALMONT, partly from Original Documents. By the Rev. G. R.
GLEIG, M.A. 8vo. with Portrait, 15s.

FATHER MATHEW: a Biography. By JOHN FRANCIS MAGUIRE,
M.P. Second Edition, with Portrait. Post 8vo. 12s. 6d.

Rome; its Ruler and its Institutions. By the same Author. New
Edition in preparation.

LIFE of AMELIA WILHELMINA SIEVEKING, from the German.
Edited, with the Author's sanction, by CATHERINE WINKWORTH. Post 8vo.
with Portrait, 12s.

FELIX MENDELSSOHN'S LETTERS from *Italy and Switzerland*,
translated by LADY WALLACE, Third Edition, with Notice of MENDELSSOHN'S Life and Works, by Henry F. CHORLEY; and *Letters from 1833 to
1847*, translated by Lady WALLACE. New Edition, with Portrait. 2 vols.
crown 8vo. 5s. each.

DIARIES of a LADY of QUALITY, from 1797 to 1844. Edited, with
Notes, by A. Hayward, Q.C. Second Edition. Post 8vo. 10s. 6d.

RECOLLECTIONS of the late WILLIAM WILBERFORCE, M.P.
for the County of York during nearly 30 Years. By J. S. HARFORD, D.C.L.
F.R.S. Post 8vo. 7s.

LIFE and CORRESPONDENCE of THEODORE PARKER. By
JOHN WEISS. With 2 Portraits and 19 Wood Engravings. 2 vols. 8vo. 30s.

SOUTHEY'S LIFE of WESLEY. Fifth Edition. Edited by the Rev.
C. C. SOUTHEY, M.A. Crown 8vo. 7s. 6d.

THOMAS MOORE'S MEMOIRS, JOURNAL, and CORRESPONDENCE. Edited and abridged from the First Edition by Earl RUSSELL.
Square crown 8vo. with 8 Portraits, 12s. 6d.

MEMOIR of the Rev. SYDNEY SMITH. By his Daughter, Lady
HOLLAND. With a Selection from his Letters, edited by Mrs. AUSTIN.
2 vols. 8vo. 28s.

LIFE of WILLIAM WARBURTON, D.D. Bishop of Gloucester from
1760 to 1779. By the Rev. J. S. WATSON, M.A. 8vo. with Portrait, 18s.

FASTI EBORACENSES: Lives of the Archbishops of York. By the
late Rev. W. H. DIXON, M.A. Edited and enlarged by the Rev. J. RAINE,
M.A. In 2 vols. Vol. I. comprising the lives to the Death of Edward III.
8vo. 15s.

VICISSITUDES of FAMILIES. By Sir BERNARD BURKE, Ulster
King of Arms. FIRST, SECOND, and THIRD SERIES. 3 vols. crown 8vo.
12s. 6d. each.

BIOGRAPHICAL SKETCHES. By NASSAU W. SENIOR. Post 8vo. price 10s. 6d.

ESSAYS in ECCLESIASTICAL BIOGRAPHY. By the Right Hon. Sir J. STEPHEN, LL.D. Fourth Edition. 8vo. 14s.

ARAGO'S BIOGRAPHIES of DISTINGUISHED SCIENTIFIC MEN. By FRANÇOIS ARAGO. Translated by Admiral W. H. SMYTH, F.R.S. the Rev. B. POWELL, M.A. and R. GRANT, M.A. 8vo. 18s.

MAUNDER'S BIOGRAPHICAL TREASURY: Memoirs, Sketches, and Brief Notices of above 12,000 Eminent Persons of All Ages and Nations. Fcp. 8vo. 10s.

Criticism, Philosophy, Polity, &c.

PAPINIAN: a Dialogue on State Affairs between a Constitutional Lawyer and a Country Gentleman about to enter Public Life. By GEORGE ATKINSON, B.A. Oxon. Serjeant-at-Law. Post 8vo. 5s.

On REPRESENTATIVE GOVERNMENT. By JOHN STUART MILL. Second Edition, 8vo. 9s.

Dissertations and Discussions. By the same Author. 2 vols. 8vo. price 24s.

On Liberty. By the same Author. Third Edition. Post 8vo. 7s. 6d.

Principles of Political Economy. By the same. Fifth Edition. 2 vols. 8vo. 30s.

A System of Logic, Ratiocinative and Inductive. By the same. Fifth Edition. Two vols. 8vo. 25s.

Utilitarianism. By the same. 8vo. 5s.

LORD BACON'S WORKS, collected and edited by R. L. ELLIS, M.A J. SPEDDING, M.A. and D. D. HEATH. Vols. I. to V. *Philosophical Works* 5 vols. 8vo. £4 6s. VOLS. VI. and VII. *Literary and Professional Works* 2 vols. £1 16s.

BACON'S ESSAYS with ANNOTATIONS. By R. WHATELY, D.D. late Archbishop of Dublin. Sixth Edition. 8vo. 10s. 6d.

ELEMENTS of LOGIC. By R. WHATELY, D.D. late Archbishop of Dublin. Ninth Edition. 8vo. 10s. 6d. crown 8vo. 4s. 6d.

Elements of Rhetoric. By the same Author. Seventh Edition. 8vo. 10s. 6d. crown 8vo. 4s. 6d.

English Synonymes. Edited by Archbishop WHATELY. 5th Edition. Fcp. 8vo. 3s.

MISCELLANEOUS REMAINS from the Common-place Book of the late Archbishop WHATELY. Edited by Miss E. J. WHATELY. Post 8vo. 6s.

ESSAYS on the ADMINISTRATIONS of GREAT BRITAIN from 1783 to 1830, contributed to the *Edinburgh Review* by the Right Hon. Sir G. C. LEWIS, Bart. Edited by the Right Hon. Sir E. HEAD, Bart. 8vo. with Portrait, 15s.

By the same Author.

A Dialogue on the Best Form of Government, 4s. 6d.

Essay on the Origin and Formation of the Romance Languages, price 7s. 6d.

Historical Survey of the Astronomy of the Ancients, 15s.

Inquiry into the Credibility of the Early Roman History, 2 vols. price 30s.

On the Methods of Observation and Reasoning in Politics, 2 vols. price 28s.

Irish Disturbances and Irish Church Question, 12s.

Remarks on the Use and Abuse of some Political Terms, 9s.

On Foreign Jurisdiction and Extradition of Criminals, 2s. 6d.

The Fables of Babrius, Greek Text with Latin Notes, PART I. 5s. 6d. PART II. 3s. 6d.

Suggestions for the Application of the Egyptological Method to Modern History, 1s.

An OUTLINE of the NECESSARY LAWS of THOUGHT: a Treatise on Pure and Applied Logic. By the Most Rev. W. THOMSON, D.D. Archbishop of York. Crown 8vo. 5s. 6d.

The ELEMENTS of LOGIC. By THOMAS SHEDDEN, M.A. of St. Peter's Coll. Cantab. Crown 8vo. [*Just ready.*

ANALYSIS of Mr. MILL'S SYSTEM of LOGIC. By W. STEBBING, M.A. Fellow of Worcester College, Oxford. Post 8vo. [*Just ready.*

SPEECHES of the RIGHT HON. LORD MACAULAY, corrected by Himself. 8vo. 12s.

LORD MACAULAY'S SPEECHES on PARLIAMENTARY REFORM in 1831 and 1832. 16mo. 1s.

A DICTIONARY of the ENGLISH LANGUAGE. By R. G. LATHAM, M.A. M.D. F.R.S. Founded on that of Dr. JOHNSON, as edited by the Rev. H. J. TODD, with numerous Emendations and Additions. Publishing in 36 Parts, price 3s. 6d. each, to form 2 vols. 4to.

The English Language. By the same Author. Fifth Edition. 8vo. price 18s.

Handbook of the English Language. By the same Author. Fourth Edition. Crown 8vo. 7s. 6d.

Elements of Comparative Philology. By the same Author. 8vo. 21s.

THESAURUS of ENGLISH WORDS and PHRASES, classified and arranged so as to facilitate the Expression of Ideas, and assist in Literary Composition. By P. M. ROGET, M. D. 11th Edition. Crown 8vo. 10s. 6d.

LECTURES on the SCIENCE of LANGUAGE, delivered at the Royal Institution. By MAX MULLER, M.A. Fellow of All Souls College, Oxford. FIRST SERIES, Fourth Edition. 8vo. 12s. SECOND SERIES, with 31 Woodcuts, price 18s.

The DEBATER; a Series of Complete Debates, Outlines of Debates, and Questions for Discussion. By F. ROWTON. Fcp. 8vo. 6s.

A COURSE of ENGLISH READING, adapted to every taste and capacity; or, How and What to Read. By the Rev. J. PYCROFT, B.A. Fcp. 8vo. 5s.

MANUAL of ENGLISH LITERATURE, Historical and Critical: with a Chapter on English Metres. By T. ARNOLD, B.A. Prof. of Eng. Lit. Cath. Univ. Ireland. Post 8vo. 10s. 6d.

SOUTHEY'S DOCTOR, complete in One Volume. Edited by the Rev. J. W. WARTER, B.D. Square crown 8vo. 12s. 6d.

HISTORICAL and CRITICAL COMMENTARY on the OLD TESTAMENT; with a New Translation. By M. M. KALISCH, Ph.D. VOL. I. *Genesis*, 8vo. 18s. or adapted for the General Reader, 12s. VOL. II. *Exodus*, 15s. or adapted for the General Reader, 12s.

A Hebrew Grammar, with Exercises. By the same. PART I. Outlines with Exercises, 8vo. 12s. 6d. KEY, 5s. PART II. *Exceptional Forms and Constructions*, 12s. 6d.

A NEW LATIN-ENGLISH DICTIONARY. By the Rev. J. T. WHITE, M.A. of Corpus Christi College, and Rev. J. E. RIDDLE, M.A. of St. Edmund Hall, Oxford. Imperial 8vo. 42s.

A Diamond Latin-English Dictionary, or Guide to the Meaning, Quality, and Accentuation of Latin Classical Words. By the Rev. J. E. RIDDLE, M.A. 32mo. 4s.

A NEW ENGLISH-GREEK LEXICON, containing all the Greek Words used by Writers of good authority. By C. D. YONGE, B.A. Fourth Edition. 4to. 21s.

A LEXICON, ENGLISH and GREEK, abridged for the Use of Schools from his 'English-Greek Lexicon' by the Author, C. D. YONGE, B.A. Square 12mo. [*Just ready.*

A GREEK-ENGLISH LEXICON. Compiled by H. G. LIDDELL, D.D. Dean of Christ Church, and R. SCOTT, D.D. Master of Balliol. Fifth Edition. Crown 4to. 31s. 6d.

A Lexicon, Greek and English, abridged from LIDDELL and SCOTT'S *Greek-English Lexicon*. Tenth Edition. Square 12mo. 7s. 6d.

A PRACTICAL DICTIONARY of the FRENCH and ENGLISH LANGUAGES. By L. CONTANSEAU. 7th Edition. Post 8vo. 10s. 6d.

Contanseau's Pocket Dictionary, French and English; being a close Abridgment of the above, by the same Author. 2nd Edition. 18mo. 5s.

NEW PRACTICAL DICTIONARY of the **GERMAN LANGUAGE;** German-English and English-German. By the Rev. W. L. BLACKLEY, M.A. and Dr. CARL MARTIN FRIEDLANDER. Post 8vo. [*In the press.*

Miscellaneous Works and Popular Metaphysics.

RECREATIONS of a COUNTRY PARSON: being a Selection of the Contributions of A. K. H. B. to *Fraser's Magazine*. SECOND SERIES. Crown 8vo. 3s. 6d.

The Common-place Philosopher in Town and Country. By the same Author. Crown 8vo. 3s. 6d.

Leisure Hours in Town; Essays Consolatory, Æsthetical, Moral, Social, and Domestic. By the same. Crown 8vo. 3s. 6d.

The Autumn Holidays of a Country Parson. By the same Author. 1 vol. [*Nearly ready.*

FRIENDS in COUNCIL: a Series of Readings and Discourses thereon. 2 vols. fcp. 8vo. 9s.

Friends in Council, SECOND SERIES. 2 vols. post 8vo. 14s.

Essays written in the Intervals of Business. Fcp. 8vo. 2s. 6d.

Companions of My Solitude. By the same Author. Fcp. 8vo. 3s. 6d.

LORD MACAULAY'S MISCELLANEOUS WRITINGS: comprising his Contributions to KNIGHT'S *Quarterly Magazine*, Articles from the Edinburgh Review not included in his *Critical and Historical Essays*, Biographies from the *Encyclopædia Britannica*, Miscellaneous Poems and Inscriptions. 2 vols. 8vo. with Portrait, 21s.

The REV. SYDNEY SMITH'S MISCELLANEOUS WORKS; including his Contributions to the *Edinburgh Review*.

LIBRARY EDITION. 3 vols. 8vo. 36s.
TRAVELLER'S EDITION, in 1 vol. 21s.
In POCKET VOLUMES. 3 vols. 21s.
PEOPLE'S EDITION. 2 vols. crown 8vo. 8s.

Elementary Sketches of Moral Philosophy, delivered at the Royal Institution. By the same Author. Fcp. 8vo. 7s.

The Wit and Wisdom of Sydney Smith: a Selection of the most memorable Passages in his Writings and Conversation. 16mo. 7s. 6d.

From MATTER to SPIRIT: the Result of Ten Years' Experience in Spirit Manifestations. By C. D. with a preface by A. B. Post 8vo. 8s. 6d.

The HISTORY of the SUPERNATURAL in All Ages and Nations, and in all Churches, Christian and Pagan; Demonstrating a Universal Faith. By WILLIAM HOWITT. 2 vols. post 8vo. 18s.

CHAPTERS on MENTAL PHYSIOLOGY. By Sir HENRY HOLLAND, Bart. M.D. F.R.S. Second Edition. Post 8vo. 8s. 6d.

ESSAYS selected from CONTRIBUTIONS to the *Edinburgh Review.* By HENRY ROGERS. Second Edition. 3 vols. fcp. 21s.

The Eclipse of Faith; or, a Visit to a Religious Sceptic. By the same Author. Tenth Edition. Fcp. 8vo. 5s.

Defence of the Eclipse of Faith, by its Author; a rejoinder to Dr. Newman's *Reply.* Third Edition. Fcp. 8vo. 3s. 6d.

Selections from the Correspondence of R. E. H. Greyson. By the same Author. Third Edition. Crown 8vo. 7s. 6d.

Fulleriana, or the Wisdom and Wit of THOMAS FULLER, with Essay on his Life and Genius. By the same Author. 16mo. 2s. 6d.

Reason and Faith, reprinted from the *Edinburgh Review.* By the same Author. Fourth Edition. Fcp. 8vo. 1s. 6d.

An INTRODUCTION to MENTAL PHILOSOPHY, on the Inductive Method. By J. D. MORELL, M.A. LL.D. 8vo. 12s.

Elements of Psychology, containing the Analysis of the Intellectual Powers. By the same Author. Post 8vo. 7s. 6d.

The SENSES and the INTELLECT. By ALEXANDER BAIN, M.A. Professor of Logic in the University of Aberdeen. Second Edition. 8vo. price 15s.

The Emotions and the Will, by the same Author; completing a Systematic Exposition of the Human Mind. 8vo. 15s.

On the Study of Character, including an Estimate of Phrenology. By the same Author. 8vo. 9s.

HOURS WITH THE MYSTICS: a Contribution to the History of Religious Opinion. By ROBERT ALFRED VAUGHAN, B.A. Second Edition. 2 vols. crown 8vo. 12s.

PSYCHOLOGICAL INQUIRIES, or Essays intended to illustrate the Influence of the Physical Organisation on the Mental Faculties. By Sir B. C. BRODIE, Bart. Fcp. 8vo. 5s. PART II. Essays intended to illustrate some Points in the Physical and Moral History of Man. Fcp. 8vo. 5s.

The PHILOSOPHY of NECESSITY; or Natural Law as applicable to Mental, Moral, and Social Science. By CHARLES BRAY. Second Edition. 8vo. 9s.

The Education of the Feelings and Affections. By the same Author. Third Edition. 8vo. 3s. 6d.

CHRISTIANITY and COMMON SENSE. By Sir WILLOUGHBY JONES, Bart. M.A. Trin. Coll. Cantab. 8vo. 6s.

Astronomy, Meteorology, Popular Geography, &c.

OUTLINES of ASTRONOMY. By Sir J. F. W. HERSCHEL, Bart. M.A. Seventh Edition, revised; with Plates and Woodcuts. 8vo. 18s.

ARAGO'S POPULAR ASTRONOMY. Translated by Admiral W. H. Smyth, F.R.S. and R. Grant, M.A. With 25 Plates and 358 Woodcuts. 2 vols. 8vo. £2 5s.

Arago's Meteorological Essays, with Introduction by Baron Humboldt. Translated under the superintendence of Major-General E. Sabine, R.A. 8vo. 18s.

The WEATHER-BOOK; a Manual of Practical Meteorology. By Rear-Admiral Robert Fitz Roy, R.N. F.R.S. Third Edition, with 16 Diagrams. 8vo. 15s.

SAXBY'S WEATHER SYSTEM, or Lunar Influence on Weather, By S. M. Saxby, R.N. Principal Instructor of Naval Engineers, H.M. Steam Reserve. Second Edition. Post 8vo. 4s.

DOVE'S LAW of STORMS considered in connexion with the ordinary Movements of the Atmosphere. Translated by R. H. Scott, M.A. T.C.D. 8vo. 10s. 6d.

CELESTIAL OBJECTS for COMMON TELESCOPES. By the Rev. T. W. Webb, M.A. F.R.A.S. With Map of the Moon, and Woodcuts. 16mo. 7s.

PHYSICAL GEOGRAPHY for SCHOOLS and GENERAL READERS. By M. F. Maury, LL.D. Author of 'Physical Geography of the Sea,' &c. Fcp. 8vo. with 2 Plates, 2s. 6d.

A DICTIONARY, Geographical, Statistical, and Historical, of the various Countries, Places, and Principal Natural Objects in the World. By J. R. M'Culloch, Esq. With 6 Maps. 2 vols. 8vo. 63s.

A GENERAL DICTIONARY of GEOGRAPHY, Descriptive, Physical, Statistical, and Historical: forming a complete Gazetteer of the World. By A. Keith Johnston, F.R.S.E. 8vo. 30s.

A MANUAL of GEOGRAPHY, Physical, Industrial, and Political. By W. Hughes, F.R.G.S. Professor of Geography in King's College, and in Queen's College, London. With 6 Maps. Fcp. 8vo. 7s. 6d.

Or in Two Parts:—Part I. Europe, 3s. 6d. Part II. Asia, Africa, America, Australasia, and Polynesia, 4s.

The Geography of British History; a Geographical description of the British Islands at Successive Periods, from the Earliest Times to the Present Day. By the same. With 6 Maps. Fcp. 8vo. 8s. 6d.

The BRITISH EMPIRE; a Sketch of the Geography, Growth, Natural and Political Features of the United Kingdom, its Colonies and Dependencies. By Caroline Bray. With 5 Maps. Fcp. 8vo. 7s. 6d.

COLONISATION and COLONIES: a Series of Lectures delivered before the University of Oxford. By Herman Merivale, M.A. Professor of Political Economy. 8vo. 18s.

The AFRICANS at HOME: a popular Description of Africa and the Africans. By the Rev. R. M. Macbrair, M.A. Second Edition; including an Account of the Discovery of the Source of the Nile. With Map and 70 Woodcuts. Fcp. 8vo. 5s.

MAUNDER'S TREASURY of GEOGRAPHY, Physical, Historical, Descriptive, and Political. Completed by W. Hughes, F.R.G.S. With 7 Maps and 16 Plates. Fcp. 8vo. 10s.

Natural History and Popular Science.

The ELEMENTS of PHYSICS or NATURAL PHILOSOPHY. By NEIL ARNOTT, M.D. F.R.S. Physician Extraordinary to the Queen. Sixth Edition. PART I. 8vo. 10s. 6d.

HEAT CONSIDERED as a MODE of MOTION; a Course of Lectures delivered at the Royal Institution. By Professor JOHN TYNDALL, F.R.S. Crown 8vo. with Woodcuts, 12s. 6d.

VOLCANOS, the Character of their Phenomena, their Share in the Structure and Composition of the Surface of the Globe, &c. By G. POULETT SCROPE, M.P. F.R.S. Second Edition. 8vo. with illustrations, 15s.

A TREATISE on ELECTRICITY, in Theory and Practice. By A. DE LA RIVE, Prof. in the Academy of Geneva. Translated by C. V. WALKER, F.R.S. 3 vols. 8vo. with Woodcuts, £3 13s.

The CORRELATION of PHYSICAL FORCES. By W. R. GROVE, Q.C. V.P.R.S. Fourth Edition. 8vo. 7s. 6d.

The GEOLOGICAL MAGAZINE; or, Monthly Journal of Geology Edited by T. RUPERT JONES, F.G.S. Professor of Geology in the R. M. College, Sandhurst; assisted by J. C. WOODWARD, F.G.S. F.Z.S. British Museum. 8vo. with Illustrations, price 1s. 6d. monthly.

A GUIDE to GEOLOGY. By J. PHILLIPS, M.A. Professor of Geology in the University of Oxford. Fifth Edition; with Plates and Diagrams. Fcp. 8vo. 4s.

A GLOSSARY of MINERALOGY. By H. W. BRISTOW, F.G.S. of the Geological Survey of Great Britain. With 486 Figures. Crown 8vo. 12s.

PHILLIPS'S ELEMENTARY INTRODUCTION to MINERALOGY, with extensive Alterations and Additions, by H. J. BROOKE, F.R.S. and W. H. MILLER, F.G.S. Post 8vo. with Woodcuts, 18s.

VAN DER HOEVEN'S HANDBOOK of ZOOLOGY. Translated from the Second Dutch Edition by the Rev. W. CLARK, M.D. F.R.S. 2 vols. 8vo. with 24 Plates of Figures, 60s.

The COMPARATIVE ANATOMY and PHYSIOLOGY of the VERTE-brate Animals. By RICHARD OWEN, F.R.S. D.C.L. 2 vols. 8vo. with upwards of 1,200 Woodcuts. [*In the press.*

HOMES WITHOUT HANDS: an Account of the Habitations constructed by various Animals, classed according to their Principles of Construction. By Rev. J. G. WOOD, M.A. F.L.S. Illustrations on Wood by G. Pearson, from Drawings by F. W. Keyl and E. A. Smith. In course of publication in 20 Parts, 1s. each.

MANUAL of CŒLENTERATA. By J. REAY GREENE, B.A. M.R.I.A. Edited by the Rev. J. A. GALBRAITH, M.A. and the Rev. S. HAUGHTON, M.D. Fcp. 8vo. with 39 Woodcuts, 5s.

Manual of Protozoa; with a General Introduction on the Principles of Zoology. By the same Author and Editors. Fcp. 8vo. with 16 Woodcuts, 2s.

Manual of the Metalloids. By J. APJOHN, M.D. F.R.S. and the same Editors. Fcp. 8vo. with 38 Woodcuts, 7s. 6d.

THE ALPS: Sketches of Life and Nature in the Mountains. By Baron H. VON BERLEPSCH. Translated by the Rev. L. STEPHEN, M.A. With 17 Illustrations. 8vo. 15s.

The SEA and its LIVING WONDERS. By Dr. G. HARTWIG. Second (English) Edition. 8vo. with many Illustrations. 18s.

The TROPICAL WORLD. By the same Author. With 8 Chromo-xylographs and 172 Woodcuts. 8vo. 21s.

SKETCHES of the NATURAL HISTORY of CEYLON. By Sir J. EMERSON TENNENT, K.C.S. LL.D. With 82 Wood Engravings. Post 8vo. price 12s. 6d.

Ceylon. By the same Author. 5th Edition; with Maps, &c. and 90 Wood Engravings. 2 vols. 8vo. £2 10s.

MARVELS and MYSTERIES of INSTINCT; or, Curiosities of Animal Life. By G. GARRATT. Third Edition. Fcp. 8vo. 7s.

HOME WALKS and HOLIDAY RAMBLES. By the Rev. C. A. JOHNS, B.A. F.L.S. Fcp. 8vo. with 10 Illustrations, 6s.

KIRBY and SPENCE'S INTRODUCTION to ENTOMOLOGY, or Elements of the Natural History of Insects. Seventh Edition. Crown 8vo. price 5s.

MAUNDER'S TREASURY of NATURAL HISTORY, or Popular Dictionary of Zoology. Revised and corrected by T. S. COBBOLD, M.D, Fcp. 8vo. with 900 Woodcuts, 10s.

The TREASURY of BOTANY, on the Plan of Maunder's Treasury. By J. LINDLEY, M.D. and T. MOORE, F.L.S. assisted by other Practical Botanists. With 16 Plates, and many Woodcuts from designs by W. H. Fitch. Fcp. 8vo. *[In the press.*

The ROSE AMATEUR'S GUIDE. By THOMAS RIVERS. 8th Edition. Fcp. 8vo. 4s.

The BRITISH FLORA; comprising the Phænogamous or Flowering Plants and the Ferns. By Sir W. J. HOOKER, K.H. and G. A. WALKER ARNOTT, LL.D. 12mo. with 12 Plates, 14s. or coloured, 21s.

BRYOLOGIA BRITANNICA; containing the Mosses of Great Britain and Ireland, arranged and described. By W. WILSON. 8vo. with 61 Plates 42s. or coloured, £4 4s.

The INDOOR GARDENER. By Miss MALING. Fcp. 8vo. with coloured Frontispiece, 5s.

LOUDON'S ENCYCLOPÆDIA of PLANTS; comprising the Specific Character, Description, Culture, History, &c. of all the Plants found in Great Britain. With upwards of 12,000 Woodcuts. 8vo. £3 13s. 6d.

Loudon's Encyclopædia of Trees and Shrubs; containing the Hardy Trees and Shrubs of Great Britain scientifically and popularly described. With 2,000 Woodcuts 8vo. 50s.

HISTORY of the BRITISH FRESHWATER ALGÆ. By A. H. HASSALL, M.D. With 100 Plates of Figures. 2 vols. 8vo. price £1 15s.

MAUNDER'S SCIENTIFIC and LITERARY TREASURY; a Popular Encyclopædia of Science, Literature, and Art. Fcp. 8vo. 10s.

A DICTIONARY of SCIENCE, LITERATURE and ART; comprising the History, Description, and Scientific Principles of every Branch of Human Knowledge. Edited by W. T. BRANDE, F.R.S.L. and E. Fourth Edition, revised and corrected. [*In the press.*

ESSAYS on SCIENTIFIC and other SUBJECTS, contributed to the *Edinburgh* and *Quarterly Reviews*. By Sir H. HOLLAND, Bart. M.D. Second Edition. 8vo. 14s.

ESSAYS from the EDINBURGH and QUARTERLY REVIEWS; with Addresses and other pieces. By Sir J. F. W. HERSCHEL, Bart, M.A. 8vo. 18s.

Chemistry, Medicine, Surgery, and the Allied Sciences.

A DICTIONARY of CHEMISTRY and the Allied Branches of other Sciences; founded on that of the late Dr. Ure. By HENRY WATTS, F.C.S. assisted by eminent Contributors. 4 vols. 8vo. in course of publication in Monthly Parts. VOL. I. 31s. 6d. and VOL. II. 26s. are now ready.

HANDBOOK of CHEMICAL ANALYSIS, adapted to the Unitary System of Notation: Based on Dr. H. Wills' *Anleitung zur chemischen Analyse.* By F. T. CONINGTON, M.A. F.C.S. Post 8vo. 7s. 6d.—TABLES of QUALITATIVE ANALYSIS to accompany the same, 2s. 6d.

A HANDBOOK of VOLUMETRICAL ANALYSIS. By ROBERT H. SCOTT, M.A. T.C.D. Post 8vo. 4s. 6d.

ELEMENTS of CHEMISTRY, Theoretical and Practical. By WILLIAM A. MILLER, M.D. LL.D. F.R.S. F.G.S. Professor of Chemistry, King's College, London. 3 vols. 8vo. £2 12s. PART I. CHEMICAL PHYSICS. Third Edition enlarged, 12s. PART II. INORGANIC CHEMISTRY. Second Edition, 20s. PART III. ORGANIC CHEMISTRY. Second Edition, 20s.

A MANUAL of CHEMISTRY, Descriptive and Theoretical. By WILLIAM ODLING, M.B. F.R.S. Lecturer on Chemistry at St. Bartholomew's Hospital. PART I. 8vo. 9s.

A Course of Practical Chemistry, for the use of Medical Students. By the same Author. PART I. crown 8vo. with Woodcuts, 4s. 6d. PART II. (completion) *just ready.*

The DIAGNOSIS and TREATMENT of the DISEASES of WOMEN; including the Diagnosis of Pregnancy. By GRAILY HEWITT, M.D. Physician to the British Lying-in Hospital. 8vo. 16s.

LECTURES on the DISEASES of INFANCY and CHILDHOOD. By CHARLES WEST, M.D. &c. Fourth Edition, revised and enlarged. 8vo. 14s.

EXPOSITION of the SIGNS and SYMPTOMS of PREGNANCY: with other Papers on subjects connected with Midwifery. By W. F. MONTGOMERY, M.A. M.D. M.R.I.A. 8vo. with Illustrations, 25s.

A SYSTEM of SURGERY, Theoretical and Practical. In Treatises by Various Authors, arranged and edited by T. HOLMES, M.A. Cantab. Assistant-Surgeon to St. George's Hospital. 4 vols. 8vo.

Vol. I. General Pathology. 21s.

Vol. II. Local Injuries—Diseases of the Eye. 21s.

Vol. III. Operative Surgery. Diseases of the Organs of Special Sense, Respiration, Circulation, Locomotion and Innervation. 21s.

Vol. IV. Diseases of the Alimentary Canal, of the Urino-genitary Organs, of the Thyroid, Mamma and Skin; with Appendix of Miscellaneous Subjects, and GENERAL INDEX. [*Early in October.*

LECTURES on the PRINCIPLES and PRACTICE of PHYSIC. By THOMAS WATSON, M.D. Physician-Extraordinary to the Queen. Fourth Edition. 2 vols. 8vo. 34s.

LECTURES on SURGICAL PATHOLOGY. By J. PAGET, F.R.S. Surgeon-Extraordinary to the Queen. Edited by W. TURNER, M.B. 8vo. with 117 Woodcuts, 21s.

A TREATISE on the CONTINUED FEVERS of GREAT BRITAIN. By C. MURCHISON, M.D. Senior Physician to the London Fever Hospital. 8vo. with coloured Plates, 18s.

DEMONSTRATIONS of MICROSCOPIC ANATOMY; a Guide to the Examination of the Animal Tissues and Fluids in Health and Disease, for the use of the Medical and Veterinary Professions. Founded on a Course of Lectures delivered by Dr. HARLEY, Prof. in Univ. Coll. London. Edited by G. T. BROWN, late Vet. Prof. in the Royal Agric. Coll. Cirencester. 8vo. with Illustrations. [*Nearly ready.*

ANATOMY, DESCRIPTIVE and SURGICAL. By HENRY GRAY, F.R.S. With 410 Wood Engravings from Dissections. Third Edition, by T. HOLMES, M.A. Cantab. Royal 8vo. 28s.

PHYSIOLOGICAL ANATOMY and PHYSIOLOGY of MAN. By the late R. B. TODD, M.D. F.R.S. and W. BOWMAN, F.R.S. of King's College. With numerous Illustrations. VOL. II. 8vo. 25s.

A New Edition of the FIRST VOLUME, by Dr. LIONEL S. BEALE, is preparing for publication.

The CYCLOPÆDIA of ANATOMY and PHYSIOLOGY. Edited by the late R. B. TODD, M.D. F.R.S. Assisted by nearly all the most eminent cultivators of Physiological Science of the present age. 5 vols. 8vo. with 2,853 Woodcuts, £6 6s.

A DICTIONARY of PRACTICAL MEDICINE. By J. COPLAND, M.D. F.R.S. Abridged from the larger work by the Author, assisted by J. C. COPLAND. 1 vol. 8vo. [*In the press.*

Dr. Copland's Dictionary of Practical Medicine (the larger work). 3 vols. 8vo. £5 11s.

The WORKS of SIR B. C. BRODIE, Bart. Edited by CHARLES HAWKINS, F.R.C.S.E. 2 vols. 8vo. [*In the press.*

MEDICAL NOTES and REFLECTIONS. By Sir H. HOLLAND, Bart. M.D. Third Edition. 8vo. 18s.

HOOPER'S MEDICAL DICTIONARY, or Encyclopædia of Medical Science. Ninth Edition, brought down to the present time, by ALEX. HENRY, M.D. 1 vol. 8vo. [*In the press.*

A MANUAL of MATERIA MEDICA and THERAPEUTICS, abridged from Dr. PEREIRA'S *Elements* by F. J. FARRE, M.D. Cantab. assisted by R. BENTLEY, M.R.C.S. and by R. WARRINGTON, F.C.S. 1 vol. 8vo.

Dr. Pereira's Elements of Materia Medica and Therapeutics. Third Edition. By A. S. TAYLOR, M.D. and G. O. REES, M.D. 3 vols. 8vo. with numerous Woodcuts, £3 15s.

The Fine Arts, and Illustrated Editions.

The NEW TESTAMENT of OUR LORD and SAVIOUR JESUS CHRIST. Illustrated with numerous Engravings on Wood from the OLD MASTERS. Crown 4to. price 63s. cloth, gilt top; or price £5 5s. elegantly bound in morocco. [*In October.*

LYRA GERMANICA; Hymns for the Sundays and Chief Festivals of the Christian Year. Translated by CATHERINE WINKWORTH: 125 Illustrations on Wood drawn by J. LEIGHTON, F.S.A. Fcp. 4to. 21s.

CATS' and FARLIE'S MORAL EMBLEMS; with Aphorisms, Adages, and Proverbs of all Nations: comprising 121 Illustrations on Wood by J. LEIGHTON, F.S.A. with an appropriate Text by R. PIGOTT. Imperial 8vo. 31s. 6d.

BUNYAN'S PILGRIM'S PROGRESS: with 126 Illustrations on Steel and Wood by C. BENNETT; and a Preface by the Rev. C. KINGSLEY. Fcp. 4to. 21s.

The HISTORY of OUR LORD, as exemplified in Works of Art: with that of His Types, St. John the Baptist, and other Persons of the Old and New Testament. By Mrs. JAMESON and Lady EASTLAKE. Being the Fourth and concluding SERIES of 'Sacred and Legendary Art;' with 31 Etchings and 281 Woodcuts. 2 vols. square crown 8vo. 42s.

In the same Series, by Mrs. JAMESON.

Legends of the Saints and Martyrs. Fourth Edition, with 19 Etchings and 187 Woodcuts. 2 vols. 31s. 6d.

Legends of the Monastic Orders. Third Edition, with 11 Etchings and 88 Woodcuts. 1 vol. 21s.

Legends of the Madonna. Third Edition, with 27 Etchings and 165 Woodcuts. 1 vol. 21s.

Arts, Manufactures, &c.

ENCYCLOPÆDIA of ARCHITECTURE, Historical, Theoretical, and Practical. By JOSEPH GWILT. With more than 1,000 Woodcuts. 8vo. 42s.

TUSCAN SCULPTORS, their Lives, Works, and Times. With Illustrations from Original Drawings and Photographs. By CHARLES C. PERKINS. 2 vols. imperial 8vo. [*In the press.*

The ENGINEER'S HANDBOOK; explaining the Principles which should guide the young Engineer in the Construction of Machinery. By C. S. LOWNDES. Post 8vo. 5s.

The ELEMENTS of MECHANISM, for Students of Applied Mechanics. By T. M. GOODEVE, M.A. Professor of Nat. Philos. in King's Coll. London. With 206 Woodcuts. Post 8vo. 6s. 6d.

URE'S DICTIONARY of ARTS, MANUFACTURES, and MINES. Re-written and enlarged by ROBERT HUNT, F.R.S. assisted by numerous gentlemen eminent in Science and the Arts. With 2,000 Woodcuts. 3 vols. 8vo. £4.

ENCYCLOPÆDIA of CIVIL ENGINEERING, Historical, Theoretical, and Practical. By E. CRESY, C.E. With above 3,000 Woodcuts. 8vo. 42s.

TREATISE on MILLS and MILLWORK. By W. FAIRBAIRN, C.E. F.R.S. With 18 Plates and 322 Woodcuts. 2 vols. 8vo. 32s. or each vol. separately, 16s.

Useful Information for Engineers. By the same Author. FIRST and SECOND SERIES, with many Plates and Woodcuts. 2 vols. crown 8vo. 21s. or each vol. separately, 10s. 6d.

The Application of Cast and Wrought Iron to Building Purposes. By the same Author. Third Edition, with Plates and Woodcuts.
[*Nearly ready.*

The PRACTICAL MECHANIC'S JOURNAL: An Illustrated Record of Mechanical and Engineering Science, and Epitome of Patent Inventions. 4to. price 1s. monthly.

The PRACTICAL DRAUGHTSMAN'S BOOK of INDUSTRIAL DESIGN. By W. JOHNSON, Assoc. Inst. C.E. With many hundred Illustrations. 4to. 28s. 6d.

The PATENTEE'S MANUAL; a Treatise on the Law and Practice of Letters Patent for the use of Patentees and Inventors. By J. and J. H. JOHNSON. Post 8vo. 7s. 6d.

The ARTISAN CLUB'S TREATISE on the STEAM ENGINE, in its various Applications to Mines, Mills, Steam Navigation, Railways and Agriculture. By J. BOURNE, C.E. Fifth Edition; with 37 Plates and 546 Woodcuts. 4to. 42s.

A Catechism of the Steam Engine, in its various Applications to Mines, Mills, Steam Navigation, Railways, and Agriculture. By the same Author. With 80 Woodcuts. Fcp. 8vo. 6s.

The STORY of the GUNS. By Sir J. EMERSON TENNENT, K.C.S. F.R.S. With 33 Woodcuts. Post 8vo. 7s. 6d.

The THEORY of WAR Illustrated by numerous Examples from History. By Lieut.-Col. P. L. MACDOUGALL. *Third Edition*, with 10 Plans. Post 8vo. 10s. 6d.

NEW WORKS PUBLISHED BY LONGMAN AND CO.   17

COLLIERIES and COLLIERS; A Handbook of the Law and leading. Cases relating thereto. By J. C. FOWLER, Barrister-at-Law. Fcp. 8vo. 6s.

The ART of PERFUMERY; the History and Theory of Odours, and the Methods of Extracting the Aromas of Plants. By Dr. PIESSE, F.C.S. Third Edition, with 53 Woodcuts. Crown 8vo. 10s. 6d.

Chemical, Natural, and Physical Magic, for Juveniles during the Holidays. By the same Author. With 30 Woodcuts. Fcp. 8vo. 3s. 6d.

The Laboratory of Chemical Wonders: a Scientific Mélange for Young People. By the same. Crown 8vo. 5s. 6d.

TALPA; or the Chronicles of a Clay Farm. By C. W. HOSKYNS, Esq. With 24 Woodcuts from Designs by G. CRUIKSHANK. 16mo. 5s. 6d.

H.R.H. the PRINCE CONSORT'S FARMS: An Agricultural Memoir. By JOHN CHALMERS MORTON. Dedicated by permission to Her Majesty the QUEEN. With 40 Wood Engravings. 4to. 52s. 6d.

Handbook of Farm Labour, Steam, Water, Wind, Horse Power, Hand Power, &c. By the same Author. 16mo. 1s. 6d.

Handbook of Dairy Husbandry; comprising the General Management of a Dairy Farm, &c. By the same. 16mo. 1s. 6d.

LOUDON'S ENCYCLOPÆDIA of AGRICULTURE: comprising the Laying-out, Improvement, and Management of Landed Property, and the Cultivation and Economy of the Productions of Agriculture. With 1,100 Woodcuts. 8vo. 31s. 6d.

Loudon's Encylopædia of Gardening: Comprising the Theory and Practice of Horticulture, Floriculture, Arboriculture, and Landscape Gardening. With 1,000 Woodcuts. 8vo. 31s. 6d.

Loudon's Encyclopædia of Cottage, Farm, and Villa Architecture and Furniture. With more than 2,000 Woodcuts. 8vo. 42s.

HISTORY of WINDSOR GREAT PARK and WINDSOR FOREST. By WILLIAM MENZIES, Resident Deputy Surveyor. Dedicated by permission to H. M. the QUEEN. With 2 Maps, and 20 Photographs by the EARL of CAITHNESS and Mr. BEMBRIDGE. Imperial folio, £8 8s.

BAYLDON'S ART of VALUING RENTS and TILLAGES, and Claims of Tenants upon Quitting Farms, both at Michaelmas and Lady-Day. Eighth Edition, adapted to the present time by J. C. MORTON.

Religious and Moral Works.

An EXPOSITION of the 39 ARTICLES, Historical and Doctrinal. By E. HAROLD BROWNE, D.D. Lord Bishop of Ely. Sixth Edition, 8vo. 16s.

The Pentateuch and the Elohistic Psalms, in reply to Bishop Colenso. By the same Author. 8vo. 2s.

Examination Questions on Bishop Browne's Exposition of the Articles. By the Rev. J. GORLE, M.A. Fcp. 3s. 6d.

FIVE LECTURES on the CHARACTER of ST. PAUL; being the Hulsean Lectures for 1862. By the Rev. J. S. HOWSON, D.D. Second Edition. 8vo. 9s.

A CRITICAL and GRAMMATICAL COMMENTARY on ST. PAUL'S Epistles. By C. J. ELLICOTT, D.D. Lord Bishop of Gloucester and Bristol. 8vo.

Galatians, Third Edition, 8s. 6d.

Ephesians, Third Edition, 8s. 6d.

Pastoral Epistles, Second Edition, 10s. 6d.

Philippians, Colossians, and Philemon, Second Edition, 10s. 6d.

Thessalonians, Second Edition, 7s. 6d.

Historical Lectures on the Life of our Lord Jesus Christ: being the Hulsean Lectures for 1859. By the same. Third Edition. 8vo. 10s. 6d.

The Destiny of the Creature; and other Sermons preached before the University of Cambridge. By the same. Post 8vo. 5s.

The Broad and the Narrow Way; Two Sermons preached before the University of Cambridge. By the same. Crown 8vo. 2s.

Rev. T. H. HORNE'S INTRODUCTION to the CRITICAL STUDY and Knowledge of the Holy Scriptures. Eleventh Edition, corrected and extended under careful Editorial revision. With 4 Maps and 22 Woodcuts and Facsimiles. 4 vols. 8vo. £3 13s. 6d.

Rev. T. H. Horne's Compendious Introduction to the Study of the Bible, being an Analysis of the larger work by the same Author. Re-edited by the Rev. JOHN AYRE, M.A. With Maps. &c. Post 8vo. 9s.

The TREASURY of BIBLE KNOWLEDGE, on the Plan of Maunder's Treasuries. By the Rev. JOHN AYRE, M.A. Fcp. 8vo. with Maps and Illustrations. [*In the press.*

The GREEK TESTAMENT; with Notes, Grammatical and Exegetical. By the Rev. W. WEBSTER, M.A. and the Rev. W. F. WILKINSON, M.A. 2 vols. 8vo. £2 4s.

 VOL. I. the Gospels and Acts, 20s.

 VOL. II. the Epistles and Apocalypse, 24s.

The FOUR EXPERIMENTS in Church and State; and the Conflicts of Churches. By Lord ROBERT MONTAGU, M.P. 8vo. 12s.

EVERY-DAY SCRIPTURE DIFFICULTIES explained and illustrated; Gospels of St. Matthew and St. Mark. By J. E. PRESCOTT, M.A. late Fellow of C. C. Coll. Cantab. 8vo. 9s.

The PENTATEUCH and BOOK of JOSHUA Critically Examined. By J. W. COLENSO, D.D. Lord Bishop of Natal. PART I. *the Pentateuch examined as an Historical Narrative.* 8vo. 6s. PART II. *the Age and Authorship of the Pentateuch Considered,* 7s. 6d. PART III. *the Book of Deuteronomy,* 8s. PART IV. *the First 11 Chapters of Genesis examined and separated, with Remarks on the Creation, the Fall, and the Deluge,* 10s. 6d.

The **LIFE** and **EPISTLES** of **ST. PAUL**. By W. J. CONYBEARE, M.A. late Fellow of Trin. Coll. Cantab. and J. S. HOWSON, D.D. Principal of the Collegiate Institution, Liverpool.

LIBRARY EDITION, with all the Original Illustrations, Maps, Landscapes on Steel, Woodcuts, &c. 2 vols. 4to. 48s.

INTERMEDIATE EDITION, with a Selection of Maps, Plates, and Woodcuts. 2 vols. square crown 8vo. 31s. 6d.

PEOPLE'S EDITION, revised and condensed, with 46 Illustrations and Maps. 2 vols. crown 8vo. 12s.

The **VOYAGE** and **SHIPWRECK** of **ST. PAUL**; with Dissertations on the Ships and Navigation of the Ancients. By JAMES SMITH, F.R.S. Crown 8vo. Charts, 8s. 6d.

HIPPOLYTUS and his **AGE**; or, the Beginnings and Prospects of Christianity. By Baron BUNSEN, D.D. 2 vols. 8vo. 30s.

Outlines of the Philosophy of Universal History, applied to Language and Religion: Containing an Account of the Alphabetical Conferences. By the same Author. 2 vols. 8vo. 33s.

Analecta Ante-Nicæna. By the same Author. 3 vols. 8vo. 42s.

THEOLOGIA GERMANICA. Translated by SUSANNAH WINKWORTH: with a Preface by the Rev. C. KINGSLEY; and a Letter by Baron BUNSEN. Fcp. 8vo. 5s.

INSTRUCTIONS in the **DOCTRINE** and **PRACTICE** of **CHRIS**tianity, as an Introduction to Confirmation. By G. E. L. COTTON, D.D. Lord Bishop of Calcutta. 18mo. 2s. 6d.

ESSAYS on **RELIGION** and **LITERATURE.** By Cardinal WISEMAN, Dr. D. ROCK, F. H. LAING, and other Writers. Edited by H. E. MANNING, D.D. 8vo.

ESSAYS and REVIEWS. By the Rev. W. TEMPLE, D.D. the Rev. R. WILLIAMS, B.D. the Rev. B. POWELL, M.A. the Rev. H. B. WILSON, B.D. C. W. GOODWIN, M.A. the Rev. M. PATTISON, B.D. and the Rev. B. JOWETT, M.A. 11th Edition. Fcp. 8vo. 5s.

MOSHEIM'S ECCLESIASTICAL HISTORY. MURDOCK and SOAMES'S Translation and Notes, re-edited by the Rev. W. STUBBS, M.A. 3 vols. 8vo. 45s.

The **GENTILE** and the **JEW** in the Courts of the Temple of Christ: an Introduction to the History of Christianity. From the German of Prof. DÖLLINGER, by the Rev. N. DARNELL, M.A. 2 vols. 8vo. 21s.

PHYSICO-PROPHETICAL ESSAYS, on the Locality of the Eternal Inheritance, its Nature and Character; the Resurrection Body; and the Mutual Recognition of Glorified Saints. By the Rev. W. LISTER, F.G.S. Crown 8vo. 6s.

BISHOP JEREMY TAYLOR'S ENTIRE WORKS: With Life by BISHOP HEBER. Revised and corrected by the Rev. C. P. EDEN, 10 vols. 8vo. £5 5s.

PASSING THOUGHTS on RELIGION. By the Author of 'Amy Herbert.' 8th Edition. Fcp. 8vo. 5s.

Thoughts for the Holy Week, for Young Persons. By the same Author. 2d Edition. Fcp. 8vo. 2s.

Night Lessons from Scripture. By the same Author. 2d Edition. 32mo. 3s.

Self-Examination before Confirmation. By the same Author. 32mo. price 1s. 6d.

Readings for a Month Preparatory to Confirmation, from Writers of the Early and English Church. By the same. Fcp. 4s.

Readings for Every Day in Lent, compiled from the Writings of Bishop JEREMY TAYLOR. By the same. Fcp. 8vo. 5s.

Preparation for the Holy Communion; the Devotions chiefly from the works of JEREMY TAYLOR. By the same. 32mo. 3s.

MORNING CLOUDS. Second Edition. Fcp. 8vo. 5s.

The Afternoon of Life. By the same Author. Second Edition. Fcp. 5s.

Problems in Human Nature. By the same. Post 8vo. 5s.

The WIFE'S MANUAL; or, Prayers, Thoughts, and Songs on Several Occasions of a Matron's Life. By the Rev. W. CALVERT, M.A. Crown 8vo. price 10s. 6d.

SPIRITUAL SONGS for the SUNDAYS and HOLIDAYS throughout the Year. By J. S. B. MONSELL, LL.D. Vicar of Egham. Third Edition. Fcp. 8vo. 4s. 6d.

HYMNOLOGIA CHRISTIANA: or, Psalms and Hymns selected and arranged in the order of the Christian Seasons. By B. H. KENNEDY, D.D. Prebendary of Lichfield. Crown 8vo. 7s. 6d.

LYRA SACRA; Hymns, Ancient and Modern, Odes and Fragments of Sacred Poetry. Edited by the Rev. B. W. SAVILE, M.A. Fcp. 8vo. 5s.

LYRA GERMANICA, translated from the German by Miss C. WINKWORTH. FIRST SERIES, Hymns for the Sundays and Chief Festivals; SECOND SERIES, the Christian Life. Fcp. 8vo. 5s. each SERIES.

Hymns from Lyra Germanica, 18mo. 1s.

LYRA EUCHARISTICA; Hymns and Verses on the Holy Communion, Ancient and Modern; with other Poems. Edited by the Rev. ORBY SHIPLEY, M.A. Second Edition, revised and enlarged. Fcp. 8vo. 7s. 6d.

Lyra Messianica; Hymns and Verses on the Life of Christ, Ancient and Modern; with other Poems. By the same Editor. Fcp. 8vo. 7s. 6d.

Lyra Mystica; Hymns and Verses on Sacred Subjects, Ancient and Modern. Forming a companion volume to the above, by the same Editor. Fcp. 8vo. [*Nearly ready.*

LYRA DOMESTICA; Christian Songs for Domestic Edification. Translated from the *Psaltery and Harp* of C. J. P. SPITTA, and from other sources, by RICHARD MASSIE. FIRST and SECOND SERIES, fcp. 8vo. price 4s. 6d. each.

The CHORALE BOOK for ENGLAND; a complete Hymn-Book in accordance with the Services and Festivals of the Church of England: the Hymns translated by Miss C. WINKWORTH; the tunes arranged by Prof. W. S. BENNETT and OTTO GOLDSCHMIDT. Fcp. 4to. 10s. 6d.

Congregational Edition. Fcp. 8vo. price 1s. 6d.

Travels, Voyages, &c.

EASTERN EUROPE and WESTERN ASIA. Political and Social Sketches on Russia, Greece, and Syria. By HENRY A. TILLEY. With 6 Illustrations. Post 8vo. 10s. 6d.

EXPLORATIONS in SOUTH-WEST AFRICA, from Walvisch Bay to Lake Ngami and the Victoria Falls. By THOMAS BAINES. 8vo. with Map and Illustrations. [*In October.*

SOUTH AMERICAN SKETCHES; or, a Visit to Rio Janeiro, the Organ Mountains, La Plata, and the Paraná. By THOMAS W. HINCHLIFF, M.A. F.R.G.S. Post 8vo. with Illustrations, 12s. 6d.

EXPLORATIONS in LABRADOR. By HENRY Y. HIND, M.A. F.R.G.S. With Maps and Illustrations. 2 vols. 8vo. 32s.

The Canadian Red River and Assinniboine and Saskatchewan Exploring Expeditions. By the same Author. With Maps and Illustrations. 2 vols. 8vo. 42s.

The CAPITAL of the TYCOON; a Narrative of a Three Years' Residence in Japan. By Sir RUTHERFORD ALCOCK, K.C.B. 2 vols. 8vo. with numerous Illustrations, 42s.

LAST WINTER in ROME and other ITALIAN CITIES. By C. R. WELD, Author of 'The Pyrenees, West and East,' &c. 1 vol. post 8vo. with a Portrait of 'STELLA,' and Engravings on Wood from Sketches by the Author. [*In the Autumn.*

AUTUMN RAMBLES in NORTH AFRICA. By JOHN ORMSBY, of the Middle Temple, Author of the 'Ascent of the Grivola,' in 'Peaks, Passes, and Glaciers.' With 13 Illustrations on Wood from Sketches by the Author. Post 8vo. 8s. 6d.

PEAKS, PASSES, and GLACIERS; a Series of Excursions by Members of the Alpine Club. Edited by J. BALL, M.R.I.A. Fourth Edition; Maps, Illustrations, Woodcuts. Square crown 8vo. 21s.—TRAVELLERS' EDITION, condensed, 16mo. 5s. 6d.

Second Series, edited by E. S. KENNEDY, M.A. F.R.G.S. With many Maps and Illustrations. 2 vols. square crown 8vo. 42s.

Nineteen Maps of the Alpine Districts, from the First and Second Series of *Peaks, Passes, and Glaciers*. Price 7s. 6d.

The **DOLOMITE MOUNTAINS**. Excursions through Tyrol, Carinthia, Carniola, aud Friuli in 1861, 1862, and 1863. By J. GILBERT and G. C. CHURCHILL, F.R.G.S. With numerous Illustrations. Square crown 8vo. 21s.

MOUNTAINEERING in 1861; a Vacation Tour. By Prof. J. TYNDALL, F.R.S. Square crown 8vo. with 2 Views, 7s. 6d.

A SUMMER TOUR in the GRISONS and ITALIAN VALLEYS of the Bernina. By Mrs. HENRY FRESHFIELD. With 2 Coloured Maps and 4 Views. Post 8vo. 10s. 6d.

Alpine Byeways; or, Light Leaves gathered in 1859 and 1860. By the same Authoress. Post 8vo. with Illustrations, 10s. 6d.

A LADY'S TOUR ROUND MONTE ROSA; including Visits to the Italian Valleys. With Map and Illustrations. Post 8vo. 11s.

GUIDE to the PYRENEES, for the use of Mountaineers. By CHARLES PACKE. With Maps, &c. and a new Appendix. Fcp. 6s.

GUIDE to the CENTRAL ALPS, including the Bernese Oberland, Eastern Switzerland, Lombardy, and Western Tyrol. By JOHN BALL, M.R.I.A. Post 8vo. with 8 Maps, 7s. 6d. or with an INTRODUCTION on Alpine Travelling, and on the Geology of the Alps, 8s. 6d. The INTRODUCTION separately, 1s.

Guide to the Western Alps. By the same Author. With an Article on the Geology of the Alps by M. E. DESOR. Post 8vo. with Maps, &c. 7s. 6d.

A WEEK at the LAND'S END. By J. T. BLIGHT; assisted by E. H. RODD, R. Q. COUCH, and J. RALFS. With Map and 96 Woodcuts. Fcp. 8vo. 6s. 6d.

VISITS to REMARKABLE PLACES: Old Halls, Battle-Fields, and Scenes Illustrative of Striking Passages in English History and Poetry. By WILLIAM HOWITT. 2 vols. square crown 8vo. with Wood Engravings, price 25s.

The RURAL LIFE of ENGLAND. By the same Author. With Woodcuts by Bewick and Williams. Medium 8vo. 12s. 6d.

Works of Fiction.

LATE LAURELS: a Tale. By the Author of 'Wheat and Tares.' 2 vols. post 8vo. 15s.

GRYLL GRANGE. By the Author of 'Headlong Hall.' Post 8vo. price 7s. 6d.

A FIRST FRIENDSHIP. [Reprinted from *Fraser's Magazine.*] Crown 8vo. 7s. 6d.

THALATTA; or, the Great Commoner: a Political Romance. Crown 8vo. 9s.

ATHERSTONE PRIORY. By L. N. COMYN. 2 vols. post 8vo. 21s.

Ellice: a Tale. By the same. Post 8vo. 9s. 6d.

The LAST of the OLD SQUIRES. By the Rev. J. W. WARTER, B.D.
Second Edition. Fcp. 8vo. 4s. 6d.

TALES and STORIES by the Author of 'Amy Herbert,' uniform Edition, each Story or Tale in a single Volume.

AMY HERBERT, 2s. 6d.	IVORS, 3s. 6d.
GERTRUDE, 2s. 6d.	KATHARINE ASHTON, 3s. 6d.
EARL'S DAUGHTER, 2s. 6d.	MARGARET PERCIVAL, 5s.
EXPERIENCE OF LIFE, 2s. 6d.	LANETON PARSONAGE, 4s. 6d.
CLEVE HALL, 3s. 6d.	URSULA, 4s. 6d.

A Glimpse of the World. By the Author of 'Amy Herbert.' Fcp. 7s. 6d.

ESSAYS on FICTION; comprising Articles on Sir W. SCOTT, Sir E. B. LYTTON, Colonel SENIOR, Mr. THACKERAY, and Mrs. BEECHER STOWE. Reprinted chiefly from the *Edinburgh, Quarterly,* and *Westminster Reviews*; with large Additions. By NASSAU W. SENIOR. Post 8vo. 10s. 6d.

The GLADIATORS: A Tale of Rome and Judæa. By G. J. WHYTE MELVILLE. Crown 8vo.

Digby Grand, an Autobiography. By the same Author. 1 vol. 5s.

Kate Coventry, an Autobiography. By the same. 1 vol. 5s.

General Bounce, or the Lady and the Locusts. By the same. 1 vol. 5s.

Holmby House, a Tale of Old Northamptonshire. 1 vol. 5s.

Good for Nothing, or All Down Hill. By the same. 1 vol. 6s.

The Queen's Maries, a Romance of Holyrood. 1 vol. 6s.

The Interpreter, a Tale of the War. By the same. 1 vol. 5s.

TALES from GREEK MYTHOLOGY. By the Rev. G. W. COX, M.A. late Scholar of Trin. Coll. Oxon. Second Edition. Square 16mo. 3s. 6d.

Tales of the Gods and Heroes. By the same Author. Second Edition. Fcp. 8vo. 5s.

Tales of Thebes and Argos. By the same Author. Fcp. 8vo. 4s. 6d.

The WARDEN: a Novel. By ANTHONY TROLLOPE. Crown 8vo. 3s. 6d.

Barchester Towers: a Sequel to 'The Warden.' By the same Author. Crown 8vo. 5s.

The SIX SISTERS of the VALLEYS: an Historical Romance. By W. BRAMLEY-MOORE, M.A. Incumbent of Gerrard's Cross, Bucks. With 14 Illustrations on Wood. Crown 8vo. 5s.

Poetry and the Drama.

MOORE'S POETICAL WORKS, Cheapest Editions complete in 1 vol. including the Autobiographical Prefaces and Author's last Notes, which are still copyright. Crown 8vo. ruby type, with Portrait, 7s. 6d. or People's Edition, in larger type, 12s. 6d.

Moore's Poetical Works, as above, Library Edition, medium 8vo. with Portrait and Vignette, 21s. or in 10 vols. fcp. 3s. 6d. each.

TENNIEL'S EDITION of MOORE'S LALLA ROOKH, with 68 Wood Engravings from original Drawings and other Illustrations. Fcp. 4to. 21s.

Moore's Lalla Rookh. 32mo. Plate, 1s. 16mo. Vignette, 2s. 6d. Square crown 8vo. with 13 Plates, 15s.

MACLISE'S EDITION of MOORE'S IRISH MELODIES, with 161 Steel Plates from Original Drawings. Super-royal 8vo. 31s. 6d.

Moore's Irish Melodies, 32mo. Portrait, 1s. 16mo. Vignette, 2s. 6d. Square crown 8vo. with 13 Plates, 21s.

SOUTHEY'S POETICAL WORKS, with the Author's last Corrections and copyright Additions. Library Edition, in 1 vol. medium 8vo. with Portrait and Vignette, 14s. or in 10 vols. fcp. 3s. 6d. each.

LAYS of ANCIENT ROME; with *Ivry* and the *Armada*. By the Right Hon. LORD MACAULAY. 16mo. 4s. 6d.

Lord Macaulay's Lays of Ancient Rome. With 90 Illustrations on Wood, Original and from the Antique, from Drawings by G. SCHARF. Fcp. 4to. 21s.

POEMS. By JEAN INGELOW. Seventh Edition. Fcp. 8vo. 5s.

POETICAL WORKS of LETITIA ELIZABETH LANDON (L. E. L.) 2 vols. 16mo. 10s.

PLAYTIME with the POETS: a Selection of the best English Poetry for the use of Children. By a LADY. Crown 8vo. 5s.

The REVOLUTIONARY EPICK. By the Right Hon. BENJAMIN DISRAELI. Fcp. 8vo. 5s.

BOWDLER'S FAMILY SHAKSPEARE, cheaper Genuine Edition, complete in 1 vol. large type, with 36 Woodcut Illustrations, price 14s. or with the same ILLUSTRATIONS, in 6 pocket vols. 5s. each.

An ENGLISH TRAGEDY; Mary Stuart, from SCHILLER; and Mdlle. De Belle Isle, from A. DUMAS,—each a Play in 5 Acts, by FRANCES ANNE KEMBLE. Post 8vo. 12s.

Rural Sports, &c.

ENCYCLOPÆDIA of RURAL SPORTS; a complete Account, Historical, Practical, and Descriptive, of Hunting, Shooting, Fishing, Racing, &c. By D. P. BLAINE. With above 600 Woodcuts (20 from Designs by JOHN LEECH). 8vo. 42s.

COL. HAWKER'S INSTRUCTIONS to YOUNG SPORTSMEN in all that relates to Guns and Shooting. Revised by the Author's Son. Square crown 8vo. with Illustrations, 18s.

NOTES on RIFLE SHOOTING. By Captain HEATON, Adjutant of the Third Manchester Rifle Volunteer Corps. Fcp. 8vo. 2s. 6d.

The DEAD SHOT, or Sportsman's Complete Guide; a Treatise on the Use of the Gun, Dog-breaking, Pigeon-shooting, &c. By MARKSMAN. Fcp. 8vo. with Plates, 5s.

The CHASE of the WILD RED DEER in DEVON and SOMERSET. By C. P. COLLYNS. With Map and Illustrations. Square crown 8vo. 16s.

The FLY-FISHER'S ENTOMOLOGY. By ALFRED RONALDS. With coloured Representations of the Natural and Artificial Insect. 6th Edition; with 20 coloured Plates. 8vo. 14s.

HANDBOOK of ANGLING : Teaching Fly-fishing, Trolling, Bottom-fishing, Salmon-fishing; with the Natural History of River Fish, and the best modes of Catching them. By EPHEMERA. Fcp. Woodcuts, 5s.

The CRICKET FIELD ; or, the History and the Science of the Game of Cricket. By J. PYCROFT, B.A. Trin. Coll. Oxon. 4th Edition. Fcp. 8vo. 5s.

The Cricket Tutor ; a Treatise exclusively Practical. By the same. 18mo. 1s.

The HORSE'S FOOT, and HOW to KEEP IT SOUND. By W. MILES, Esq. 9th Edition, with Illustrations. Imp. 8vo. 12s. 6d.

A Plain Treatise on Horse-Shoeing. By the same Author. Post 8vo. with Illustrations, 2s.

General Remarks on Stables, and Examples of Stable Fittings. By the same. Imp. 8vo. with 13 Plates, 15s.

Remarks on Horses' Teeth, adapted to Purchasers. By the same Author. Crown 8vo. 1s. 6d.

The HORSE; with a Treatise on Draught. By WILLIAM YOUATT. New Edition, revised and enlarged. 8vo. with numerous Woodcuts, 10s. 6d.

The Dog. By the same Author. 8vo. with numerous Woodcuts, 6s.

The DOG in HEALTH and DISEASE. By STONEHENGE. With 70 Wood Engravings. Square crown 8vo. 15s.

The Greyhound. By the same. With many Illustrations. Square crown 8vo. 21s.

The OX ; his Diseases and their Treatment: with an Essay on Parturition in the Cow. By J. R. DOBSON, M.R.C.V.S. Post 8vo. with Illustrations.
[Just ready.

Commerce, Navigation, and Mercantile Affairs.

The LAW of NATIONS Considered as Independent Political Communities. By TRAVERS TWISS, D.C.L. Regius Professor of Civil Law in the University of Oxford. 2 vols. 8vo. 30s. or separately, PART I. *Peace*, 12s. PART II. *War*, 18s.

A DICTIONARY, Practical, Theoretical, and Historical, of Commerce and Commercial Navigation. By J. R. M'CULLOCH, Esq. 8vo. with Maps and Plans, 50s.

The STUDY of STEAM and the **MARINE ENGINE**, for Young Sea Officers. By S. M. SAXBY, R.N. Post 8vo. with 87 Diagrams, 5s. 6d.

A NAUTICAL DICTIONARY, defining the Technical Language relative to the Building and Equipment of Sailing Vessels and Steamers, &c. By ARTHUR YOUNG. Second Edition; with Plates and 150 Woodcuts. 8vo. 18s.

A MANUAL for NAVAL CADETS. By J. M'NEIL BOYD, late Captain R.N. Third Edition; with 240 Woodcuts and 11 coloured Plates. Post 8vo. 12s. 6d.

*** Every Cadet in the Royal Navy is required by the Regulations of the Admiralty to have a copy of this work on his entry into the Navy.

Works of Utility and General Information.

MODERN COOKERY for PRIVATE FAMILIES, reduced to a System of Easy Practice in a Series of carefully-tested Receipts. By ELIZA ACTON. Newly revised and enlarged; with 8 Plates, Figures, and 150 Woodcuts. Fcp. 8vo. 7s. 6d.

On FOOD and its DIGESTION; an Introduction to Dietetics. By W. BRINTON, M.D. Physician to St. Thomas's Hospital, &c. With 48 Woodcuts. Post 8vo. 12s.

ADULTERATIONS DETECTED; or Plain Instructions for the Discovery of Frauds in Food and Medicine. By A. H. HASSALL, M.D. Crown 8vo. with Woodcuts, 17s. 6d.

The VINE and its FRUIT, in relation to the Production of Wine. By JAMES L. DENMAN. Crown 8vo. 8s. 6d.

WINE, the VINE, and the CELLAR. By THOMAS G. SHAW. With 28 Illustrations on Wood. 8vo. 16s.

A PRACTICAL TREATISE on BREWING; with Formulæ for Public Brewers, and Instructions for Private Families. By W. BLACK. 8vo. 10s. 6d.

SHORT WHIST; its Rise, Progress, and Laws; with the Laws of Piquet, Cassino, Ecarté, Cribbage, and Backgammon. By Major A. Fcp. 8vo. 3s.

HINTS on ETIQUETTE and the USAGES of SOCIETY; with a Glance at Bad Habits. Revised, with Additions, by a LADY of RANK. Fcp. 8vo. 2s. 6d.

The CABINET LAWYER; a Popular Digest of the Laws of England, Civil and Criminal. 19th Edition, extended by the Author; including the Acts of the Sessions 1862 and 1863. Fcp. 8vo. 10s. 6d.

The PHILOSOPHY of HEALTH; or, an Exposition of the Physiological and Sanitary Conditions conducive to Human Longevity and Happiness. By SOUTHWOOD SMITH, M.D. Eleventh Edition, revised and enlarged: with New Plates, 8vo. [*Just ready.*]

HINTS to MOTHERS on the MANAGEMENT of their HEALTH during the Period of Pregnancy and in the Lying-in Room. By T. BULL, M.D. Fcp. 8vo. 5s.

The Maternal Management of Children in Health and Disease. By the same Author. Fcp. 8vo. 5s.

NOTES on HOSPITALS. By FLORENCE NIGHTINGALE. Third Edition, enlarged; with 13 Plans. Post 4to. 18s.

C. M. WILLICH'S POPULAR TABLES for ascertaining the Value of Lifehold, Leasehold, and Church Property, Renewal Fines, &c.; the Public Funds; Annual Average Price and Interest on Consols from 1731 to 1861; Chemical, Geographical, Astronomical, Trigonometrical Tables, &c. Post 8vo. 10s.

THOMSON'S TABLES of INTEREST, at Three, Four, Four and a Half, and Five per Cent. from One Pound to Ten Thousand and from 1 to 365 Days. 12mo. 3s. 6d.

MAUNDER'S TREASURY of KNOWLEDGE and LIBRARY of Reference: comprising an English Dictionary and Grammar, a Universal Gazetteer, a Classical Dictionary, a Chronology, a Law Dictionary, a Synopsis of the Peerage, useful Tables, &c. Fcp. 8vo. 10s.

General and School Atlases.

An ELEMENTARY ATLAS of HISTORY and GEOGRAPHY, from the commencement of the Christian Era to the Present Time, in 16 coloured Maps, chronologically arranged, with illustrative Memoirs. By the Rev. J. S. BREWER, M.A. Royal 8vo. 12s. 6d.

SCHOOL ATLAS of PHYSICAL, POLITICAL, and COMMERCIAL GEOGRAPHY, in 17 full-coloured Maps, accompanied by descriptive Letterpress. By E. HUGHES, F.R.A.S. Royal 8vo. 10s. 6d.

BISHOP BUTLER'S ATLAS of ANCIENT GEOGRAPHY, in a Series of 24 full-coloured Maps, accompanied by a complete Accentuated Index. New Edition, corrected and enlarged. Royal 8vo. 12s.

BISHOP BUTLER'S ATLAS of MODERN GEOGRAPHY, in a Series of 33 full-coloured Maps, accompanied by a complete Alphabetical Index. New Edition, corrected and enlarged. Royal 8vo. 10s. 6d.

IN consequence of the rapid advance of geographical discovery, and the many recent changes, through political causes, in the boundaries of various countries, it has been found necessary thoroughly to revise this long-established Atlas, and to add several new MAPS. New MAPS have been given of the following countries: *Palestine, Canada,* and the adjacent provinces of *New Brunswick, Nova Scotia,* and *Newfoundland,* the *American States* bordering on the Pacific, *Eastern Australia,* and *New Zealand.* In addition to these MAPS of *Western Australia* and *Tasmania* have been given in compartments; thus completing the revision of the MAP of *Australasia,* rendered necessary by the rising importance of our Australasian possessions. In the MAP of *Europe, Iceland* has also been re-drawn, and the new boundaries of *France, Italy,* and *Austria* represented. The MAPS of the three last-named countrie have been carefully revised. The MAP of *Switzerland* has been wholly re-drawn, showing more accurately the physical features of the country. *Africa* has been carefully compared with the discoveries of LIVINGSTONE, BURTON, SPEKE, BARTH, and other explorers. The number of MAPS is thus raised from Thirty to Thirty-three. An entirely new INDEX has been constructed; and the price of the work has been reduced from 12s. to Half-a-Guinea. The present edition, therefore, will be found much superior to former ones; and the Publishers feel assured that it will maintain the character which this work has so long enjoyed as a popular and comprehensive School Atlas.

MIDDLE-CLASS ATLAS of GENERAL GEOGRAPHY, in a Series of 29 full-coloured Maps, containing the most recent Territorial Changes and Discoveries. By WALTER M'LEOD, F.R.G.S. 4to. 5s.

PHYSICAL ATLAS of GREAT BRITAIN and IRELAND; comprising 30 full-coloured Maps, with illustrative Letterpress, forming a Concise Synopsis of British Physical Geography. By WALTER M'LEOD, F.R.G.S. Fcp. 4to. 7s. 6d.

Periodical Publications.

The EDINBURGH REVIEW, or CRITICAL JOURNAL, published Quarterly in January, April, July, and October. 8vo. price 6s. each No.

The GEOLOGICAL MAGAZINE, or Monthly Journal of Geology, edited by T. RUPERT JONES, F.G.S. assisted by HENRY WOODWARD, F.G.S. 8vo. price 1s. 6d. each No.

FRASER'S MAGAZINE for TOWN and COUNTRY, published on the 1st of each Month. 8vo. price 2s. 6d. each No.

The ALPINE JOURNAL: a Record of Mountain Adventure and Scientific Observation. By Members of the Alpine Club. Edited by H. B. GEORGE, M.A. Published Quarterly, May 31, Aug. 31, Nov. 30, Feb. 28. 8vo. price 1s. 6d. each No.

INDEX.

Acton's Modern Cookery 26
Afternoon of Life 20
Alcock's Residence in Japan 21
Alpine Guide (The) 22
———— Journal (The) 28
Arjohn's Manual of the Metalloids........ 11
Arago's Biographies of Scientific Men 5
———— Popular Astronomy 10
———— Meteorological Essays 10
Arnold's Manual of English Literature.... 7
Arnott's Elements of Physics.............. 11
Atherstone Priory 23
Atkinson's Papinian 5
Autumn Holidays of a Country Parson.... 8
Ayre's Treasury of Bible Knowledge...... 18

Bacon's Essays, by Whately 5
———— Life and Letters, by Spedding...... 3
———— Works, by Ellis Spedding, and Heath 5
Bain on the Emotions and Will............ 9
———— on the Senses and Intellect......... 9
———— on the Study of Character.......... 9
Baines's Explorations in S. W. Africa 21
Ball's Guide to the Central Alps 22
———— Guide to the Western Alps......... 22
Bayldon's Rents and Tillages............. 17
Beallrson's Life and Nature in the Alps... 12
Black's Treatise on Brewing 26
Blackley and Friedlander's German and English Dictionary 8
Blaine's Rural Sports 24
Blight's Week at the Land's End 22
Bourne's Catechism of the Steam Engine.. 16
———— Treatise on the Steam Engine ... 16
Bowdler's Family Shakspeare............. 24
Boyd's Manual for Naval Cadets........... 26
Bramley-Moore's Six Sisters of the Valleys 23
Brande's Dictionary of Science, Literature, and Art, ... 13
Bray's (C.) Education of the Feelings ... 9
———— Philosophy of Necessity......... 9
———— (Mrs.) British Empire........... 10
Brewer's Atlas of History and Geography 27
Brinton on Food and Digestion............ 26
Bristow's Glossary of Mineralogy......... 11
Brodie's (Sir C. B.) Psychological Inquiries 9
———— Works............................ 14
Brown's Demonstrations of Microscopic Anatomy 14
Browne's Exposition of the 39 Articles.... 17
———— Pentateuch and Elohistic Psalms 17
Buckle's History of Civilization 2
Bull's Hints to Mothers................... 27
———— Maternal Management of Children. 27

Bunsen's Analecta Ante-Nicæna 19
———— Ancient Egypt 3
———— Hippolytus and his Age 19
———— Philosophy of Universal History 19
Bunyan's Pilgrim's Progress, illustrated by Bennett 15
Burke's Vicissitudes of Families 4
Butler's Atlas of Ancient Geography 27
———— Modern Geography 28

Cabinet Lawyer 27
Calvert's Wife's Manual 20
Cats and Farlie's Moral Emblems 15
Chorale Book for England 21
Colenso (Bishop) on Pentateuch and Book of Joshua 18
Collyns on Stag-Hunting in Devon and Somerset 25
Commonplace Philosopher in Town and Country 8
Companions of my Solitude 8
Conington's Handbook of Chemical Analysis 13
Contanseau's Pocket French and English Dictionary 7
———— Practical ditto 7
Conybeare and Howson's Life and Epistles of St. Paul 19
Copland's Dictionary of Practical Medicine 11
———— Abridgment of ditto 14
Cotton's Introduction to Confirmation ... 19
Cox's Tales of the Great Persian War 2
———— Tales from Greek Mythology 23
———— Tales of the Gods and Heroes ... 23
———— Tales of Thebes and Argos 23
Cresy's Encyclopædia of Civil Engineering 16
Crowe's History of France 2

D'Aubigné's History of the Reformation in the time of Calvin..................... 2
Dead Shot (The), by Marksman 25
De la Rive's Treatise on Electricity 11
Densman's Vine and its Fruit 26
De Tocqueville's Democracy in America.. 2
Diaries of a Lady of Quality 4
Disraeli's Revolutionary Epick........... 24
Dixon's Fasti Eboracenses 4
Dobson on the Ox 25
Döllinger's Introduction to History of Christianity 19
Dove's Law of Storms 10
Doyle's Chronicle of England............ 2

NEW WORKS PUBLISHED BY LONGMAN AND CO.

Edinburgh Review (The) 28
Ellice, a Tale 23
ELLICOTT's Broad and Narrow Way 18
——— Commentary on Ephesians 18
——— Destiny of the Creature....... 18
——— Lectures on Life of Christ 18
——— Commentary on Galatians 18
——————————Pastoral Epist... 18
——————————Philippians, &c.. 18
——————————Thessalonians... 18
Essays and Reviews 19
Essays on Religion and Literature, edited by MANNING 19
Essays written in the Intervals of Business 8

FAIRBAIRN's Application of Cast and Wrought Iron to Building............. 16
——— Information for Engineers... 16
——— Treatise on Mills & Millwork 16
First Friendship 22
FITZ ROY's Weather Book 10
FORSTER's Life of Sir John Eliot......... 3
FOWLER's Collieries and Colliers......... 17
Fraser's Magazine 28
FRESHFIELD's Alpine Byways 22
——— Tour in the Grisons.......... 22
Friends in Council 8
From Matter to Spirit 8
FROUDE's History of England 1

GARRATT's Marvels and Mysteries of Instinct 12
Geological Magazine 11, 28
GILBERT and CHURCHILL's Dolomite Mountains 22
GOODEVE's Elements of Mechanism 16
GORLE's Questions on BROWNE's Exposition of the 39 Articles................. 17
GRAY's Anatomy 14
GREENE's Manual of Coelenterata.......... 11
——— Manual of Protozoa........... 11
GROVE on Correlation of Physical Forces.. 11
Gryll Grange 22
GWILT's Encyclopædia of Architecture 15

Handbook of Angling, by EPHEMERA 25
HARTWIG's Sea and its Living Wonders.... 12
——— Tropical World 12
HASSALL's Adulterations Detected 26
——— British Freshwater Algæ 12
HAWKER's Instructions to Young Sportsmen 25
HEATON's Notes on Rifle Shooting 25
HELPS's Spanish Conquest in America..... 2
HERSCHEL's Essays from the Edinburgh and Quarterly Reviews 13
——— Outlines of Astronomy 9
HEWITT on the Diseases of Women 13
HINCHLIFF's South American Sketches 21
HIND's Canadian Exploring Expeditions... 21
——— Explorations in Labrador 21
Hints on Etiquette....................... 27
HOLLAND's Chapters on Mental Physiology 8
——— Essays on Scientific Subjects... 13
——— Medical Notes and Reflections.. 15
HOLMES's System of Surgery............... 14
HOOKER and WALKER-ARNOTT's British Flora 12
HOOPER's Medical Dictionary 15
HORNE's Introduction to the Scriptures ... 18
——— Compendium of ditto.......... 18
HOSKYNS' Talpa 17
HOWITT's History of the Supernatural 8
——— Rural Life of England......... 22
——— Visits to Remarkable Places.... 22

HOWSON's Hulsean Lectures on St. Paul.... 18
HUGHES's (E.) Atlas of Physical, Political and Commercial Geography............. 7
——— (W.) Geography of British History 10
——— Manual of Geography 10
HULLAH's History of Modern Music........ 3
Hymns from *Lyra Germanica*............. 20

INGELOW's Poems.......................... 21

JAMESON's Legends of the Saints and Martyrs................................. 15
——— Legends of the Madonna...... 15
——— Legends of the Monastic Orders 15
JAMESON and EASTLAKE's History of Our Lord 15
JOHNS's Home Walks and Holiday Rambles 12
JOHNSON's Patentee's Manual 16
——— Practical Draughtsman......... 16
JOHNSTON's Gazetteer, or Geographical Dictionary 10
JONES's Christianity and Common Sense.... 9

KALISCH's Commentary on the Old Testament 7
——— Hebrew Grammar.............. 7
KEMBLE's Plays 24
KENNEDY's Hymnologia Christiana 20
KIRBY and SPENCE's Entomology 12

Lady's Tour Round Monte Rosa 22
LANDON's (L. E. L.) Poetical Works...... 24
Late Laurels 22
LATHAM's Comparative Philology.......... 6
——— English Dictionary 6
——— Handbook of the English Language................................. 5
——— Work on the English Language 6
Leisure Hours in Town 24
LEWES's Biographical History of Philosophy 4
Lewis on the Astronomy of the Ancients ... 5
——— on the Credibility of Early Roman History................................. 6
——— Dialogue on Government 6
——— on Egyptological Method....... 6
——— Essays on Administrations 6
——— Fables of BABRIUS.............. 6
——— on Foreign Jurisdiction 6
——— on Irish Disturbances......... 6
——— on Observation and Reasoning in Politics............................... 6
——— on Political Terms 6
——— on the Romance Languages..... 6
LIDDELL and SCOTT's Greek-English Lexicon
——— Abridged ditto 7
LINDLEY and MOORE's Treasury of Botany 12
LISTER's Physico-Prophetical Essays 19
LONGMAN's Lectures on the History of England 2
LOUDON's Encyclopædia of Agriculture.... 17
——— Cottage, Farm, and Villa Architecture 17
——— Gardening..... 17
——— Plants....... 12
——— Trees & Shrubs 12
LOWNDES's Engineer's Handbook 16
Lyra Domestica 21
——— Eucharistica 20
——— Germanica................... 15, 20
——— Messianica 20
——— Mystica...................... 20
——— Sacra 20

NEW WORKS PUBLISHED BY LONGMAN AND CO. 31

MACAULAY's (Lord) Essays 3
——————History of England 1
——————Lays of Ancient Rome 21
——————Miscellaneous Writings 8
——————Speeches 6
——————Speeches on Parliamentary Reform..................................... 6
MACBRAIR's Africans at Home 10
MACDOUGALL's Theory of War............. 16
McLEOD's Middle-Class Atlas of General Geography 28
——————Physical Atlas of Great Britain and Ireland 29
McCULLOCH's Dictionary of Commerce 26
——————Geographical Dictionary...... 10
AGUIRE's Life of Father Mathew.......... 4
——————Rome and its Rulers......... 4
MALING's Indoor Gardener 12
Maps from Peaks, Passes, and Glaciers ... 16
MARSHALL's History of Christian Missions. 3
ASSEY's History of England 1
AUNDER's Biographical Treasury 5
——————Geographical Treasury 10
——————Historical Treasury 3
——————Scientific and Literary Treasury 13
——————Treasury of Knowledge 27
——————Treasury of Natural History .. 12
MAURY's Physical Geography 10
MAY's Constitutional History of England.. 1
MELVILLE's Digby Grand.................... 23
——————General Bounce 23
——————Gladiators 23
——————Good for Nothing............. 23
——————Holmby House 23
——————Interpreter 23
——————Kate Coventry 23
——————Queen's Maries................ 23
MENDELSSOHN's Letters.................... 4
MENZIES' Windsor Great Park............ 17
MERIVALE's (H. Colonisation and Colonies 10
——————(C.) Fall of the Roman Republic 2
——————Romans under the Empire 2
MERYON's History of Medicine............ 3
MILES on Horse's Foot 25
——————On Horses' Teeth 25
——————on Horse Shoeing.............. 25
——————on Stables................... 25
MILL on Liberty........................... 5
——————on Representative Government.. 5
——————on Utilitarianism............. 5
MILL's Dissertations and Discussions 5
——————Political Economy 5
——————System of Logic 5
MILLER's Elements of Chemistry......... 13
MONSELL's Spiritual Songs 20
MONTAGU's Experiments in Church and State...................................... 18
MONTGOMERY on the Signs and Symptoms of Pregnancy................................ 13
MOORE's Irish Melodies.................... 21
——————Lalla Rookh 21
——————Memoirs, Journal, and Correspondence.................................. 4
——————Poetical Works............... 24
MORELL's Elements of Psychology 9
——————Mental Philosophy 9
Morning Clouds 20
MORTON's Handbook of Dairy Husbandry.. 17
——————Farm Labour............. 17
——————Prince Consort's Farms....... 17
MOSHEIM's Ecclesiastical History 19
MÜLLER's (Max) Lectures on the Science of Language................................... 7
——————(K. O.) Literature of Ancient Greece 2
MURCHISON on Continued Fevers......... 11
MURE's Language and Literature of Greece 2

New Testament illustrated with Wood Engravings from the Old Masters............ 15
NEWMAN's Apologia pro Vitâ Suâ 3
NIGHTINGALE's Notes on Hospitals......... 27

ODLING's Course of Practical Chemistry 13
——————Manual of Chemistry 13
ORMSBY's Rambles in Algeria and Tunis.... 21
OWEN's Comparative Anatomy and Physiology of Vertebrate Animals 11

PACKE's Guide to the Pyrenees 22
PAGET's Lectures on Surgical Pathology... 14

PARKER's (Theodore) Life, by WEISS........ 4
Peaks, Passes, and Glaciers, 2 Series 21
PEREIRA's Elements of Materia Medica.... 15
——————Manual of Materia Medica 15
PERKINS's Tuscan Sculptors 16
PHILLIPS's Guide to Geology 11
——————Introduction to Mineralogy 11
PIESSE's Art of Perfumery 17
——————Chemical, Natural, and Physical Magic 17
——————Laboratory of Chemical Wonders 17
Playtime with the Poets 24
Practical Mechanic's Journal 16
PRESCOTT's Scripture Difficulties 18
Problems in Human Nature................. 20
PYCROFT's Course of English Reading...... 7
——————Cricket Field 25
——————Cricket Tutor 25

Recreations of a Country Parson, SECOND SERIES 8
RIDDLE's Diamond Latin-English Dictionary 7
RIVERS's Rose Amateur's Guide............ 12
ROGERS's Correspondence of Greyson 9
——————Eclipse of Faith 9
——————Defence of ditto 9
——————Essays from the Edinburgh Review 9
——————Fullerians.................. 9
——————Reason and Faith............. 9
ROGET's Thesaurus of English Words and Phrases................................... 5
RONALDS's Fly-Fisher's Entomology 25
ROWTON's Debater......................... 7

Saxby's Study of Steam 26
――― Weather System.................. 10
Scott's Handbook of Volumetrical Analysis 13
Scrope on Volcanos 11
Senior's Biographical Sketches 5
――― Essays on Fiction 23
Sewell's Amy Herbert 23
――― Ancient History 2
――― Cleve Hall....................... 23
――― Earl's Daughter................. 23
――― Experience of Life.............. 23
――― Gertrude 23
――― Glimpse of the World 23
――― History of the Early Church..... 3
――― Ivors........................... 23
――― Katharine Ashton 23
――― Laneton Parsonage............... 23
――― Margaret Percival 23
――― Night Lessons from Scripture 20
――― Passing Thoughts on Religion.... 20
――― Preparation for Communion 20
――― Readings for Confirmation....... 20
――― Readings for Lent 20
――― Self-Examination before Confirmation 20
――― Stories and Tales 23
――― Thoughts for the Holy Week 20
――― Ursula 23
Shaw's Work on Wine 26
Shedden's Elements of Logic 6
Short Whist 26
Sieveking's (Amelia) Life, by Winkworth 4
Smith's (Southwood) Philosophy of Health 27
――― (J.) Voyage and Shipwreck of St. Paul 19
――― (G.) Wesleyan Methodism........ 3
――― (Sydney) Memoir and Letters 4
――― ――― Miscellaneous Works 8
――― ――― Sketches of Moral Philosophy............................. 8
――― ――― Wit and Wisdom 8
Southey's (Doctor) 7
――― Poetical Works................. 24
Steebing's Analysis of Mill's Logic........ 6
Stephenson's (R.) Life by Jeaffreson and Pole 3
Stephen's Essays in Ecclesiastical Biography............................. 5
――― Lectures on the History of France 2
Stonehenge on the Dog 25
――― on the Greyhound............. 25
Strickland's Queens of England 1

Theologia Germanica 19
Thirlwall's History of Greece 2
Thomson's (Archbishop) Laws of Thought 5
――― (J.) Tables of Interest 27
Tilley's Eastern Europe and Western Asia 21
Todd's Cyclopædia of Anatomy and Physiology 14
――― and Bowman's Anatomy and Physiology of Man 14
Trollope's Barchester Towers............. 23
――― Warden 23
Twiss's Law of Nations 26
Tyndall's Lectures on Heat............... 11
――― Mountaineering in 1861......... 22

Ure's Dictionary of Arts, Manufactures, and Mines 16

Vander Hoeven's Handbook of Zoology.. 11
Vaughan's (R.) Revolutions in English History............................. 1
――― (R. A.) Hours with the Mystics 9
Warburton's Life, by Watson 4
Warter's Last of the Old Squires......... 23
Watson's Principles and Practice of Physic 14
Watts's Dictionary of Chemistry......... 13
Webb's Celestial Objects for Common Telescopes 10
Webster & Wilkinson's Greek Testament 18
Weld's Last Winter in Rome............. 21
Wellington's Life, by Brialmont and Gleig 4
――― by Gleig 4
Wesley's Life, by Southey 4
West on the Diseases of Infancy and Childhood 13
Whately's English Synonymes 5
――― Logic 5
――― Remains 5
――― Rhetoric 5
Whewell's History of the Inductive Sciences 2
White and Riddle's Latin-English Dictionary 7
Wilberforce (W.) Recollections of, by Harford 4
Willich's Popular Tables 27
Wilson's Bryologia Britannica 12
Wood's Homes without Hands........... 11
Woodward's Historical and Chronological Encyclopædia 3

Taylor's (Jeremy) Works, edited by Eden 19
Tennent's Ceylon 12
――― Natural History of Ceylon...... 12
――― Story of the Guns 16
Thalatta 22

Yonge's English-Greek Lexicon 7
――― Abridged ditto 7
Young's Nautical Dictionary 26
Youatt on the Dog 25
――― on the Horse 25

www.ingramcontent.com/pod-product-compliance
Lightning Source LLC
Chambersburg PA
CBHW020927230426
43666CB00008B/1596